An Economist's Lessons on Happiness

Richard A. Easterlin

An Economist's Lessons on Happiness

Farewell Dismal Science!

Consulting editor Nancy L. Easterlin

 Springer

Richard A. Easterlin
Pasadena, CA, USA

ISBN 978-3-030-61961-9   ISBN 978-3-030-61962-6   (eBook)
https://doi.org/10.1007/978-3-030-61962-6

This Springer imprint is published by the registered company Springer Nature Switzerland AG
The registered company address is: Gewerbestrasse 11, 6330 Cham, Switzerland

For my wife, my children, and my grandchildren
Who make me very happy

Preface

I sit here, stunned. The government of Australia is proposing to restructure college tuition charges so as to encourage enrollment in STEM subjects (science, technology, engineering, and mathematics) at the expense of the humanities and social sciences. Apparently, the ongoing professionalization of higher education is not enough. It seems that we need less of what this book is about and even bigger container ships.

I write as one who has had a foot in both camps. My undergraduate education and initial work experience were as a mechanical engineer. My graduate education was in economics and, as an economist, I have specialized in economic history, demography, and now, happiness, often straying beyond the confines of economics. In my view, our lives and dealing with the world around us depend on the humanities and social sciences as much as or more than the Stem disciplines, necessary as they are. In case you think this judgment is just "sour grapes," the whining of someone who barely stumbled through engineering, I humbly note that I was the valedictorian of my undergraduate class.

Personal happiness is a near-universal aspiration, and governments everywhere proclaim their intent to advance the well-being of the population. But what to do? This book is the answer of a social scientist. It does not pretend to be the last word on the subject. I leave it to the reader to decide whether I should have stayed in engineering.

In writing the book, I have had the benefit as consulting editor of my daughter, Nancy Easterlin, University Research Professor of English Literature at the University of New Orleans, whose help went well beyond correcting my text. Nancy pointed out many passages needing clarification and illustration and did much to enliven and expand the classroom interactions. My thanks too to her husband, Peter McNamara, for his suggestions, based on a careful reading of an initial draft.

Kelsey J. O'Connor was typically helpful in drawing the graphs and configuring the illustrations, as well as providing comments. I am grateful to the Gallup World Poll for data access, and to John F. Helliwell who provided several helpful tabulations from the Poll. My daughter, Molly, helped with my multiple computer problems and Susan Lennon at Alamy with my struggles with stock photos. Johannes Glaeser and Judith Kripp of Springer Nature patiently fielded numerous queries. Finally, my thanks to those whose pictures brighten the volume.

Pasadena, California   Richard A. Easterlin
August 2020

Contents

Brief Biographies

 **Richard A. Easterlin** is University Professor Emeritus of Economics, University of Southern California. He is a member of the National Academy of Sciences and a Distinguished Fellow of the American Economic Association. He is also a Fellow of the American Academy of Arts and Sciences, the Econometric Society, and the Institute for the Study of Labor (IZA) and is a former president of the Population Association of America, Economic History Association, and Western Economic Association International. He is the author, among other things, of *Happiness, Growth and the Life Cycle* (2010), *The Reluctant Economist* (2004), *Growth Triumphant: The 21ˢᵗ Century in Historical Perspective* (1996), and *Birth and Fortune: The Impact of Numbers on Personal Welfare* (1980; 2ⁿᵈ ed. 1987), and editor of *Happiness in Economics* (2002).

Nancy L. Easterlin is University Research Professor of English and Professor of Women's and Gender Studies at the University of New Orleans, where she has taught since 1991. A pioneer of cognitive-evolutionary approaches to literature, Nancy is author of *A Biocultural Approach to Literary Theory and Interpretation* (Johns Hopkins, 2012) and *Wordsworth and the Question of "Romantic Religion"* (1996) as well as numerous essays on cognitive-evolutionary theory and literary interpretation. She is guest editor of several journal issues, including, most recently, "Knowledge, Understanding, Well-

Being: Cognitive Literary Studies" (*Poetics Today*, 2019). Her current research applies the interdisciplinary area of *place studies* to literary interpretation.

Richard and Nancy L. Easterlin were the first father and daughter to have been selected for Guggenheim Fellowships in the history of the foundation (1988–89 and 2008, respectively).

List of Figures

List of Tables

1

Introduction

1.1 The Path Via Paradox

Although economics has come a long way since T. R. Malthus' prophecies of doom, it still retains the taint of the "dismal science." But the emergence in the last half century of happiness as a legitimate subject of economic inquiry may put to rest this characterization, because the economics of happiness demonstrates that people's everyday lives can be significantly improved.

I was there at the start, the first economist to study happiness statistics—the "father of happiness economics." I was trying to figure out whether the data indicated that more money increases happiness. The result was the discovery of the paradox of happiness and income—what has come to be called the "Easterlin Paradox" (more on that in Chap. 3). But the Paradox is only one of a growing number of discoveries about happiness made by me and an increasing number of scholars attracted to this new field of study. The aim of this book is to share with you some of the lessons I have learned about happiness, in the hope that it will benefit you as it has me. It's my personal interpretation, one that draws especially on the work of my research collaborators and me; you can bet that not all happiness scholars will agree with everything I say.

It is only since World War II that happiness has moved into the social sciences. Nearly all of the earlier literature is in the humanities, going all the way back to Aristotle. This work typically takes off from preconceived ideas about what *should* make people happy—what makes for the Good Life. On this, there are almost as many judgments as judges. Although there is much thought-provoking wisdom in this literature, it doesn't offer solid evidence about how happy people really are and what *does* make them happy, which is

© The Author(s), under exclusive license to Springer Nature Switzerland AG 2021
R. A. Easterlin, *An Economist's Lessons on Happiness*,
https://doi.org/10.1007/978-3-030-61962-6_1

what the social scientist seeks to know. Now, for the first time, thanks to public opinion surveys, we have well-tested data and credible real-world evidence that tell us what the principal sources of people's happiness are and how happiness can be increased.

To me, economics is about people and their well-being. Yet not all economists share this view, and whether happiness has a place in the discipline remains even today a moot question. Back in the early nineteenth century, however, when economics was founded, the relevance of happiness was not an issue: Happiness was a centerpiece of the new discipline, and the public's well-being was its ultimate concern. Economists of the Classical School, such as David Ricardo, James Mill, and his son, John Stuart Mill, held to Jeremy Bentham's "Greatest Happiness Principle": "Utility, or the Greatest Happiness Principle, holds that actions are right … as they tend to promote happiness, wrong as they tend to produce the reverse of happiness" (John Stuart Mill (1957) [1861] p. 77. See also Fig. 1.1, especially Item 4).

Throughout the nineteenth century, economists continued to think and talk in quantitative terms about utility and happiness; however, no measure for these conjoined factors was identified. Perhaps Anglo-Irish economist Francis Edgeworth came the closest. In his 1881 volume, *Mathematical Psychics*, he advanced the notion of a "hedonimeter," a device to measure utility. But there was no practical result.

The discipline's attitude toward happiness took a sharp turn for the worse around the start of the twentieth century. Italian economist Vilfredo Pareto played a pivotal part, *asserting that economics is not about well-being; rather, the proper focus of economics is decision-making*. In his view, economics is a science of choice, not one of outcomes. Pareto was one of the pioneers in formalizing

1. Recognizes the fundamental role of Pain and Pleasure in human life.

2. Approves or disapproves of an action on the basis of the amount of pain or pleasure brought about ("consequences")

3. Equates the good with the pleasurable and evil with pain.

4. Asserts that pleasure and pain are capable of "quantification" – and hence of measure.

Fig. 1.1 The principle of utility and sketch of Jeremy Bentham's mummified corpse (Courtesy of Robert Cavalier, Carnegie Mellon University)

economic analysis. Singing his praises at mid-century, Benoit Mandelbrot and Richard L. Hudson write:

> His legacy as an economist was profound. Partly because of him, the field evolved from a branch of moral philosophy as practiced by Adam Smith into a data intensive field of scientific research and mathematical equations. His books look more like modern economics than most other texts of that day: tables of statistics from across the world and ages, rows of integral signs and equations, intricate charts and graphs. (Mandelbrot and Hudson 2004, 153)

Pareto's view of the purpose of the discipline—economics as a science of choice—came to rule twentieth-century economics. Happiness was summarily dismissed and, with it, human beings. The primary focus of economic analysis became the production, distribution, and consumption of goods. People were reduced to "factors of production." Well-being, if mentioned at all, was simply assumed to vary directly with the per person supply of goods. As Mariano Rojas puts it, "Economists who were trained in the first half of the twentieth century learned almost nothing about people's happiness; instead they mastered a highly sophisticated framework to study people's decisions and to explain market-equilibrium quantities and prices." (Rojas 2019, 9).

Speaking personally, I can attest to the truth of this: "Been there; done that."

Enter, toward the start of this century, the economics of happiness—a return to studying real people and their well-being, but for the first time with actual measures of happiness. Not for all economists, of course—not even for a majority. Nonetheless, the proportion of happiness scholars is increasing steadily. Economics is getting back to the good old days, when people were human beings with real, recognized feelings, not mere agents or factors of production. Now we can measure happiness and learn, in Jeremy Bentham's words, about their pleasure and pain.

So, let's get to it. I focus first, in Part I, on the question in the forefront of every reader's mind: How can I increase my happiness? My answer is simpler than most—some would say, too simple—but I try to make my reasoning clear. Part II takes up a parallel question: Can the government increase people's happiness? And, if so, *should* the government try to increase happiness? Part III addresses a wide-ranging set of concerns that people have about happiness: "What happens as we get older?", "Who are happier, women or men?", "Why are some countries happier than others?", "Does democracy matter?", and many, many more. Part IV draws on my earlier life as an economic historian and demographer and tries to put the mounting work on happiness in historical perspective.

Much that I cover here is from an undergraduate course on the economics of happiness that I've taught in recent years. As is always true of teaching, I have profited greatly from what my students have taught me. For this, thank you all for teaching and learning along with me.

References

Mandelbrot, B., & Hudson, R. L. (2004). *The (mis)behavior of markets: A fractal view of risk, ruin, and reward*. New York: Basic Books.

Mill, J. S. (1957) [1861]. *Utilitarianism*. Ed. Oskar Piest. Indianapolis, IN: Bobbs-Merrill.

Rojas, M. (2019). The relevance of Richard A. Easterlin's groundbreaking work: A historical perspective. In M. Rojas (Ed.), *The economics of happiness* (pp. 3–23). Basel, Switzerland: Springer Nature.

Part I

First Lessons

2

Measuring Happiness

2.1 Happiness Yardsticks

The students straggle in and plop down in their seats. We're off and running—well, jogging, maybe.

The United States is not the happiest country in the world, not even close. The top ten consists chiefly of the Nordic countries plus Canada, Australia, and New Zealand. The United States barely makes the second 10, coming in at number 18, slightly ahead of the United Kingdom. So say the data in the 2019 *World Happiness Report*, published annually since 2012 under the auspices of the United Nations (Helliwell, Layard & Sachs 2019).

If you're wondering how we measure happiness, you're not alone. It's where we start in my class as soon as any measures of happiness are mentioned.

So, we measure happiness by questioning people about their feelings. Shortly after World War II, public opinion researchers started asking questions like: "Taking all things together, how would you say things are these days—would you say you are very happy, pretty happy, or not too happy?" This type of question about *overall happiness* has since been included in surveys all over the world and is still a standard query in the US General Social Survey, which dates from 1972.

Subsequently, researchers have devised similar questions with a larger number of response options, and researchers use these widely. For example, the World Values Survey asks about *life satisfaction*: "All things considered, how satisfied are you with your life as a whole these days?" The Survey offers integer response options from 1 (=Dissatisfied) to 10 (=Satisfied). The principal measure in the *World Happiness Report*, which is the basis of the country

© The Author(s), under exclusive license to Springer Nature Switzerland AG 2021
R. A. Easterlin, *An Economist's Lessons on Happiness*,
https://doi.org/10.1007/978-3-030-61962-6_2

rankings just mentioned, is from the Gallup World Poll, which uses a best-worst question. People are asked to rate their lives on a *ladder-of-life* scale from 0 to 10, where 0, at the bottom of the ladder, equals, in their view, the worst possible life and 10, the top rung, equals the best.

In the happiest countries, answers to the ladder-of-life question average seven or more; responses in the least happy countries are in the range of 3–4. You may think this is not a very big difference, but consider this. In India, where happiness averages around four, only 8.6% of respondents report values of seven or higher. In the three happiest countries (Finland, Denmark, and Norway), the percentage reporting seven or more is almost ten times greater, 85%.

So, where do *you* stand on the ladder of life? Think about the best possible life for you (=10) and the worst possible life (=0).

What is your answer?

If your answer is 7 or more, you're with the 70% of US respondents who answer similarly. Another 10% say "6," and 11% answer "5." (I do hope you're not with the 9% whose answer is less than 5.)

These questions on overall happiness, life satisfaction, and ladder-of-life are currently grouped together under the rubric *subjective well-being*. But for brevity, I'll use the more self-evident term "happiness" to refer to all three measures. People have no trouble answering questions about their happiness (did you?); the non-response rate is typically negligible.

At this point in my class, the floodgates open.Lily leads off. "But what good are these answers? People's moods change all the time." She shifts her gaze sidewise. "You know, someone might feel pretty good today, but not so much tomorrow. And forget about next week."

"Not only that," chimes in Ted, "How do you know that people are telling you how they really feel? Maybe they don't want to admit that they're unhappy."

"Yes, and also," adds Jill, "Do Lily and Ted mean the same thing by 'happiness'? I don't think so. What makes you think you can compare the happiness of different people? Averaging their responses as though they have the same idea of happiness makes no sense to me."

These are good, hard questions. Let's take up each in turn.

2.2   Short-Lived Ups and Downs?

Lily's concern is that a person's happiness response depends on his or her particular mood when the question is asked, and moods fluctuate hourly, daily, and from 1 week to the next. Maybe the respondent feels grumpy right now, and the answer reflects this passing frame of mind.

Moods are, indeed, highly variable, but the happiness questions ask about one's overall state of life, not how respondents feel at the moment. And psychologists have found that, when asked a state-of-life question, people's answers, if not always exactly the same, change fairly little on a daily or weekly basis.

Here's how they check on this, what psychologists call the "reliability" of the responses. They use a "test-retest procedure," surveying the same people several times over the course of a few days or weeks to see how consistent the individual responses are. For the three happiness questions I just described, they usually find that those who say that they are happy in the first survey also tend to be happy in subsequent surveys; unhappy respondents are also largely consistently unhappy. I've found the same is true in previous undergraduate classes when I survey the students in several successive weeks. This does not mean that respondents, -students and non-students, give exactly the same answer in each survey. Some may shift from 7 to 6 or 8, but very few move to less than 5, and few of those who start off below 5 jump to 6 or 7. Although moods may fluctuate a lot, it seems that respondents understand that the happiness questions ask about their lives in general, not their momentary moods, and these overall evaluations of their lives change relatively little in the short-term. So, the evidence indicates that the answers to the happiness questions are, in fact, "reliable."

Additionally, psychologists have developed separate survey questions aimed specifically at identifying temporary moods. For example, researchers ask, "In the last 24 h, how frequently were you angry: most of the time, some of the time, a little of the time, or not at all?" Note that the time period in this question is "the last 24 h," so the query is getting specifically at short-lived states of mind. Replace "angry," with words like "sad," "depressed," "cheerful," and the like—not to mention "happy"—and you begin to get a sense of the wide range of emotions such surveys cover. Measures of momentary moods shouldn't be confused, however, with state-of-life judgments expressed in answers about general happiness, satisfaction with life, and standing on a ladder-of-life. Questions about life in general are *evaluative measures*, because they are asking the respondent to step back and assess his or her life as a whole; those about momentary moods are *experiential measures*, because they refer to very recent experience.

Here's an illustration of the difference between evaluative and experiential measures of happiness. My wife and I are on an overnight flight from Los Angeles to Paris, where we plan to embark on a 1-week vacation cruise. In the seats behind us are a pair of merrymakers, partying all night and making sleep impossible. The next day in the lobby of our Paris hotel, an intrepid survey interviewer grabs me and, among other things, asks, "Taking all things together, how would you say things are these days—would you say you are very happy, pretty happy, or not too happy?" Considering my situation on the whole—in Paris with my wife and bound for a river cruise—I'd doubtlessly say, "very happy." But suppose the interviewer had asked instead, "In the last 24 h how frequently were you happy—most of the time, some of the time, a little of the time, or not at all?" Given my perpetual state of annoyance during the flight, I would have answered, at best, "a little of the time." The first question is evaluative, asking about my general state of life; the second question is experiential, asking about my mood on the previous day.

My focus here is on the evaluative measures, and these measures are generally reliable. As one would expect, the experiential measures are, by contrast, pretty volatile.

2.3   Telling It Like It Is?

Did you fudge your reply?

This is Ted's concern: that people may not say how they really feel—they won't admit, for instance, that they are unhappy. Psychologists have been hard at work on this question, too. To evaluate the truthfulness of happiness responses—their so-called validity—psychologists compare a person's self-reported happiness with the evaluations of those who know the respondent well, spouses or partners, relatives, friends, co-workers, and the like. It turns out that those who say they're happy are also happy in the eyes of others, and "not happy" reports are confirmed by others as well.

Similarly, clinical evaluations generally correlate positively with respondents' self-reports: Those identified by clinicians as depressed normally say that they're unhappy. The validity of self-reported happiness is also supported by correlations with facial expressions. "Very happy" respondents smile and laugh more often. And physiological measures of brain waves and stress further confirm self-reports of happiness. Taking all this together, it seems that people are telling interviewers how they really do feel, whether happy or unhappy, and to what degree.

My undergraduates don't dissemble—and I doubt that you did, either.

2.4   Different Things to Different People?

Still, even if each person is truthful and gives consistent answers from 1 week to the next, how can we compare the happiness of different people? This is what Jill wants to know.

Comparability is a problem too in international comparisons like those in the *World Happiness Report* we discussed earlier. Happiness may mean different things in different cultures. Happiness in a largely Muslim country like Indonesia may not mean the same as in a multicultural country like the United States.

Jill's question puts her in special company. In the discipline of economics, comparability surfaces in debates about the feasibility of *interpersonal comparisons of utility*. (In our lingo, *interpersonal comparisons of happiness*.) In economics, the assumption has been: Nope, not possible—what makes your neighbor happy isn't what makes you happy. Far from it. Comparisons are off limits!

But solid empirical data suggest that comparability may not be as big a problem as it seems at first glance. It turns out that the sources of happiness are much the same for most people all over the world. The most comprehensive evidence of this comes from a survey of individuals in 13 countries worldwide—rich and poor, communist and noncommunist—conducted back in the early 1960s by social psychologist Hadley Cantril. In face-to-face interviews, researchers asked people first to describe fully what really mattered to them personally—to imagine the future in the best possible light, if they were to be perfectly happy. An analogous question asked about their fears and worries—to imagine the future in the worst possible light. They were then presented with a ladder-of-life, with rungs from 0 to 10, on which 10 is the best possible life and 0 the worst, and they were asked on which rung they presently stood.

"Hold on, professor—that's the Gallup Poll ladder-of-life question, right?" asks Ted.

I know it seems the same, but there's an important difference. This handout gives the specific questions asked in both the Gallup and Cantril surveys (see Table 2.1).

Table 2.1 Ladder-of-life questions compared: Gallup World Poll and Hadley Cantril survey (Course handout #1)

Gallup world poll
Please imagine a ladder with steps numbered from 0 at the bottom to 10 at the top. Suppose we say that the top of the ladder represents the best possible life for you and the bottom of the ladder represents the worst possible life for you. On which step of the ladder would you say you personally feel you stand at this time, assuming that the higher the step, the better you feel about your life, and the lower the step, the worse you feel about it? Which step comes closest to the way you feel?
Hadley Cantril survey
(A) All of us want certain things out of life. When you think about what really matters in your own life, what are your wishes and hopes for the future? In other words, if you imagine your future in the *best* possible light, what would your life look like then, if you were to be happy? Take your time in answering; such things aren't easy to put into words
Permissible probes: What are your hopes for the future? What would your life have to be like for you to be completely happy? What is missing for you to be happy? (use also, if necessary, the words "dreams" and "desires.")
Obligatory probe: Anything else?
(B) Now, taking the other side of the picture, what are your fears and worries about the future? In other words, if you imagine your future in the *worst* possible light, what would your life look life then? Again, take your time in answering
Permissible probes: What would make you unhappy? (stress the words "fears" and "worries.")
Obligatory probe: Anything else?
(C) Here is a picture of a ladder. Suppose we say that the top of the ladder (*researcher pointing*) represents the best possible life for you and the bottom (*researcher pointing*) represents the worst possible life for you
Where on the ladder (*researcher moving finger rapidly up and down ladder*) do you feel you personally stand at the *present* time? Rung number? _____

Note that in Cantril's survey, respondents have to stop and think before they then describe verbally both the best and worst of all possible worlds. Here, for example, is an agricultural laborer's response in India to the question about the best possible life for him:

> I want a son and a piece of land since I am now working on land owned by other people. I would like to construct a house of my own and have a cow for milk and ghee. I would also like to buy some better clothing for my wife. If I could do this, then I would be happy. (Cantril 1965, 206)

In the Gallup survey, no such antecedent description of the best possible life is included; all that respondents need to say is where they stand on the ladder-of-life. You can see that Cantril's survey provides valuable insight into what people are thinking about when they rate their happiness.

The open-endedness of the questions in Cantril's work is truly pathbreaking. Respondents are free to say anything and describe as many circumstances affecting their happiness as they wish. Hence, the questions elicit a wealth of information about best and worst possible lives—what comes to mind when asked about the sources of their happiness. In this respect, the study was and still is a striking departure from the norm. Often, in survey questions of this type, respondents receive a set list of choices. Here's an example. The Organisation for Economic Cooperation and Development (OECD), a leader in promoting government surveys of happiness, published a paper in 2018 entitled "What Matters the Most to People?" The OECD offers a preconceived list of 11 possible answers, and, therefore, what matters most to respondents must be one or more of these 11 items chosen by statisticians. No doubt the statisticians do their best to read people's minds, but they are likely to come up short. For instance, the 11-item list does not include any mention of family circumstances, which, as we'll see, is one of the things that really do matter to most people. In contrast to the OECD approach, Cantril's survey never steers respondents in particular directions.

Surprisingly, the open-ended answers in Cantril's survey have received much less attention than they deserve. But I'll return to them time and time again in subsequent classes.

Although Cantril's survey is open-ended, there is remarkable consistency in the responses. Everyday circumstances, the things to which most peoples' time is devoted everywhere in the world and that they think they have some ability to control, are what people describe as important for their personal happiness. Leading the list *in every country* are three items: economic concerns, family circumstances, and health. Mentioned most frequently, often by as much as 80% of the population, are things relating to one's economic situation—concerns about the standard of living, work, or leisure time. Next in importance, cited by around 40–50% of the population, are matters relating to family circumstances—good family relationships and concerns about one's children. Named just about as frequently are issues regarding the health of oneself and one's family. Concerns about these three things—economic situation, family, and health—are by far the topics people most frequently mention when they are asked what's important for their happiness.

Broad social and political issues that are remote from most people's daily lives and that they have little ability to influence personally, such as freedom of speech, socioeconomic inequality, and international relations, aren't usually mentioned, catastrophes like war aside. Rather, it is the circumstances that occupy folks' daily lives everywhere and that they think they have some capacity to deal with that are important for happiness. Detailed types of concern—say, the particular content of "economic situation"—may differ among countries. Thus, in an agricultural society, it might be "owning a farm of one's own," in an industrial country, "a job that offers good opportunity for advancement." But a person's economic situation in general, whatever the specifics, tops the list everywhere of what people say is important for their happiness, with family and health concerns next. It is this worldwide similarity in the sources of happiness that justifies happiness comparisons—that, in economists' jargon, validates interpersonal comparisons of utility. In evaluating their happiness, most people are using the same criteria: They are thinking chiefly about their economic situation, family circumstances, and/or health. Because of the predominance everywhere of these considerations in self-reported happiness, they are my primary focus throughout the course.

In our classes, I generalize based on average relationships, as do the other researchers I cite. The observation here about the worldwide similarity in the sources of happiness derives from averages. Certainly, there are differences from one person to the next in what specifically makes for happiness. But when we study groups of people, or aggregates—rich and poor, men and women, Americans and Indonesians—these differences typically average out, and the result is dominated by the very large proportion of persons for whom the sources of happiness are essentially the same.

2.5   Subjective Vs. Objective Measures of Well-Being

"Well, in all my other economics courses," says Ted, "when they talk about well-being, they mean income. It's a straightforward measure, to me. It avoids all these problems. So why not stick with it?"

The answer, Ted, is that we're learning how to measure well-being better. Until recently, a person's well-being was judged, as you've noted, solely on the basis of so-called objective data, observations obtained from sources other than the individual's personal assessment. Economists especially have been prone to use objective measures, because, as we'll see later, they have been reluctant to credit what people say, their so-called self-reports. The assumption has been that an increase in income tells us a person is better off. Note that the individual studied doesn't select the measure or render the conclusion. By contrast, the approach of happiness economics and the resulting data it produces are an entirely new departure, based as they are on the judgment of the persons whose well-being is being evaluated. Because the individual is the one and only source of information, happiness measures are termed *subjective measures*.

It would be convenient if objective measures provided accurate insight into how well off people actually feel. Doubt that this was true was an important motivation behind the development of subjective measures like happiness. Social psychologist Angus Campbell, a pioneer in work on subjective measures, made his skepticism of objective data explicit:

> I cannot feel satisfied that the correspondence between such *objective* measures as amount of money earned … and the *subjective satisfaction* with [this] condition of life is close enough to warrant accepting the one as replacement for the other. (Campbell 1972, 448, emphasis added)

Indeed, we now know that objective and subjective measures of well-being can literally go in opposite directions. As we'll see, in China in the 1990s, incomes went up, but people's satisfaction with their lives went down. For economists, committed as they are to using objective measures, this is frustrating (Fig. 2.1). To paraphrase the late welfare economist E. J. Mishan:

> There is a temptation … to lose patience with human cussedness and to insist that if both the Wang family and the Zheng family receive a 10 per cent increase in their 'real' income, they are better off … but … if welfare is what people

Fig. 2.1 Economist having close encounter with subjective measures (Credit: Deagreez/ iStock photos)

experience, there is no escape in honest indignation. (Mishan 1969, 821, emphasis added)

In short, if people say that they are feeling no better off or (perish the thought) are feeling worse off, even though their incomes are higher and they are buying more, then who are we, the observers, to contradict them?

Indeed, as we shall see, there may be good psychological reasons why people may not feel better off, despite having more money and more material goods. So, Ted, if our aim is to determine how well off people really feel, objective measures like income are an unreliable guide, and subjective measures are needed for an accurate answer.

In happiness economics, your feelings are what counts.

2.6   The Best Measure?

Tyler's hand shoots up. "O.K., so that's interesting. But there's this measure, and then that measure—which is the best?"

Good question, Tyler. I've talked of three global measures of people's subjective well-being—overall happiness, life satisfaction, and ladder-of-life. Which best assesses people's true feelings? A tricky question, because there's no clear-cut answer. My judgment is that it really doesn't matter very much. For the well-being issues that interest most of us, the different measures usually give the same results.

Here's an illustration. Suppose we're interested in whether poverty has gone up or down. I like to reference a statistical table published quite a while ago by the US Census Bureau that presents estimates of 15 different measures of the poverty rate (yes, 15!) for 12 successive years. In any single year, the measures of those in poverty range in value from a low of 10% to a high of more than twice that value. But while the point-of-time measures differ substantially, the answer to whether and how much poverty went up or down from 1 year to the next or over longer periods is much the same, irrespective of the measure chosen. For example, from 1979 to 1983, every 1 of the 15 measures indicates that the poverty rate increased, and by just about the same amount; the smallest percentage change was 2.9, and the largest was 3.8. In short, all 15 measures agree that the poverty rate went up by about 3%.

Likewise, the three measures of subjective well-being give somewhat different point-of-time answers, but similar pictures of the change in happiness over time, of happiness differences among groups in the population such as rich and poor, and of statistical relationships. It is topics such as these that really interest us. To say, for example, that happiness in the United States is 7.4 on a scale of 0–10 doesn't mean much to most people, but to report that happiness has significantly decreased gets their attention.

Research on the best measure of subjective well-being is no doubt worthwhile, but because of the similarity in the stories the different measures tell, there's no need to single out one as the best and discard the others. Rather, it is preferable to take advantage of whatever measure the available surveys use, and that's what I do.

So, let's see what these measures tell us about what makes people happy.

References and Further Reading

Campbell, A. (1972). Aspirations, satisfaction, and fulfilment. In A. Campbell & P. E. Converse (Eds.), *The human meaning of social change* (pp. 441–466). New York: Russell Sage.

Cantril, H. (1965). *The pattern of human concerns*. New Brunswick, NJ: Rutgers University Press.

Helliwell, J. F., Layard, R., & Sachs, J. D. (Eds.). (2019). *World happiness report 2019* (pp. 13–47). New York, NY: Sustainable Solutions Network.

Helliwell, J. F., & Wang, S. (2013). The state of world happiness. In J. F. Helliwell, R. Layard, & J. D. Sachs (Eds.), *World happiness report* (pp. 10–57). New York, NY: Earth Institute of Columbia University.

Kapteyn, A., Lee, J., Tassot, C., Vonkova, H., & Zamarro, G. (2015). Dimensions of subjective well-being. *Social Indicators Research, 123*, 625–660.

Mishan, E. J. (1969). *Welfare economics: Ten introductory essays*. New York, NY: Random House.

3

Does Money Make People Happy?

3.1 The Happiness-Income Paradox

The class is once again seated. Today, we're off with a quote from our 33rd president.

As Harry S. Truman famously put it, "Give me a one-handed economist. All my economists say, 'on the one hand … but on the other.'"

If I ask you: "Will more income make you happier?" Chances are you'll say "yes." And "yes" is the almost universal response to this question in national surveys. People of all stripes think that greater happiness goes with more money. But that's what people think, and sometimes what they think turns out to be wrong. To answer the question satisfactorily, what we need are *data* about people's happiness and income, so we can see whether and how the two move together.

Enter Harry Truman. He would not be pleased with the evidence-based answer here, because half the data, it turns out, offers less than half the story. On the one hand, there are people's responses at a given point in time (*cross-section data*); on the other, there are responses at different dates (*time-series data*)—and the two give quite different answers. In cross-section data, people with higher income are happier, but in time-series data, increasing income is not accompanied by greater happiness. There are always exceptions to the rule—we all know some people with higher incomes who are unhappy. But I'm speaking here of the average or typical relationship. Again, throughout our discussions, this will be the basis of generalizations about what makes for happiness.

© The Author(s), under exclusive license to Springer Nature Switzerland AG 2021
R. A. Easterlin, *An Economist's Lessons on Happiness*,
https://doi.org/10.1007/978-3-030-61962-6_3

The positive point-of-time association between happiness and income is true not only when we look at persons within a country but also when we compare countries to one another: Richer countries are typically happier than poorer. *Over time*, however, countries with more rapid growth in income do not have a greater increase in happiness, so say the time-series data.

So, let's think a little more about the difference between cross-section and time-series. Cross-section studies, whether for individuals or countries, compare happiness and income in a survey taken at a given date. Time-series inquiries, by contrast, study happiness and income data collected in successive surveys of the same persons or group of persons, usually year after year.

In cross-section studies, then, the effect of increased income on happiness isn't determined by what actually happens to a person's happiness as his or her income goes up or down. Instead, the income-happiness relationship is decided by how the happiness of a person with a given amount of income compares with that of others with larger or smaller income. In the words of University of Michigan sociologist Arland Thornton, cross-section studies amount to "reading history sideways."

Why is there a problem with cross-section research, with studies that try to figure out what happens to a person *over time* by studying differences among persons at *a point in time*? Let's make this concrete. Suppose that in the single year 2010 everyone named Mary has more money and is happier than everyone named John. This point-of-time difference between the Marys and Johns is taken to mean that if the incomes of the Johns increase from 2010 to 2011, their happiness will go up.

Yet, as Sam sings, "The fundamental things apply/*As time goes by*."

In effect, cross-section studies stop the clock. So, to find out what really happens to happiness as people's incomes change, we need time-series data that follow the same persons or group of persons from one point in time to the next as their incomes change. Undoubtedly, time-series analysis is preferable to cross-section studies, because we are observing what really happens to happiness as people's incomes actually do go up or down. In terms of the simplistic example above, a time-series analysis would survey all the Johns in both 2010 and 2011 and, based on data for 2 years, see whether their happiness and income actually do move together.

The answer? Time-series studies say they do not—the Johns have more income, but they aren't happier.

Unfortunately, analysts are less prone to do time-series than cross-section research, because it has more problems, particularly in matters of consistency in response options. For example, suppose that in year 1 the happiness question has response options of "very happy," "pretty happy," and "not too happy" but that in year 2 the middle option, "pretty happy," is replaced with "fairly happy." Then, even if everyone's happiness is actually the same in both years, the change in wording would alter how many people choose the middle option and give an artificial impression of a change in happiness, when actually there is none. Such shifts in response options do sometimes occur in the survey questionnaire from one source to another or from 1 year to the next. Because of comparability problems like this, many researchers shy away from time-series analysis and focus on cross-section research. However, I rely primarily on time-series research, but the time-series generalizations I make are based on data that have been vetted to ensure that the happiness responses are comparable over time.

The initial time-series finding that happiness in a country does not go up as income increases was based on data for the United States alone, because it was the only country with a lengthy time series in the 1974 benchmark study. However, subsequent studies established this as the typical result. As more and more happiness data gradually accumulated, other developed countries exhibited the same nil result, and eventually nations transitioning from socialism to capitalism as well as less developed countries corroborated and thus underscored this finding. The longest time series now available is that for the United States, where the long-term trend in happiness has been flat or even declining over a 70-year period in which incomes in real terms have tripled.

So, there you have it: On the one hand, the cross-section data suggest that the answer to the question whether higher income leads to greater happiness is "yes"; on the other, the time-series data say "no." Harry Truman would go through the ceiling.

A contradiction between cross-section and time-series results is unusual but not unprecedented in economics. A similar puzzle, the *savings-income paradox*, was the source of considerable economic debate a number of years ago. In this case, research showed that, in cross-section data, as income goes up, savings as a percentage of income increases. Over time, however, the savings-to-income percentage remains fairly constant, despite an upward trend in income. To put this in terms of our illustration above, in cross-section data, all the Marys have higher income than all the Johns and save a higher percentage of their incomes. However, over time, as the incomes of both Johns and Marys increase, neither group saves a greater percentage of its income.

The happiness-income pattern is strikingly like that of the savings-income paradox—a positive cross-section relationship and nil time-series association. Hence, the *happiness-income (Easterlin) paradox*:

> At a point in time, happiness varies positively with income, both within and among nations; over time, however, the trend in happiness is not positively related to the trend in income.

Note that it is the *trends* in happiness and income—the long-run tendencies—that are not related. In the short run, happiness and income typically go up and down together. The Great Recession of 2007–2009 provides a recent example of the short-run relationship. As American incomes hit the skids, happiness plunged to the lowest level ever recorded. Then, with the economy's subsequent recovery, happiness improved. Countries in Europe and Latin America for which happiness data are available on a yearly basis display similar concurrent short-run movements in happiness and income.

What is the difference between short and long run? Here's an illustration. During an office visit, the doctor asks Derek, "Have you been watching your weight?"

Derek responds proudly, "Yup! And I've lost 2 pounds."

"That's good," says the doctor, checking his records, "but right now you're 5 pounds heavier than when I saw you at this time last year."

Derek conveniently sticks to short-run observations, whereas the doctor is looking at the long run. In the short run, Derek's weight goes up and down, and his answer reflects only the recent downside movement. It's true, as far as it goes. The doctor is discounting the short-run ups and downs and trying to identify the long-run tendency in Derek's weight—that is, the trend.

We can see short- and long-run relationships between happiness and income in Fig. 3.1.

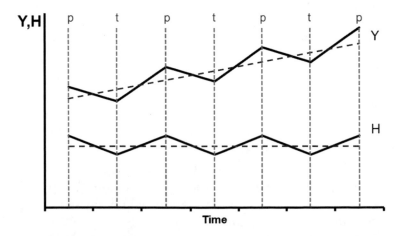

Fig. 3.1 Short-term fluctuations and long-term trends in happiness and income: An illustration (Handout #2)

Note that the peaks and troughs ('p's and 't's) in both happiness and income occur simultaneously. Thus, in the short-run relationship (the solid lines), happiness and income are fluctuating together. But if we fit a trend line to each series to identify the long-run tendency (the broken lines), it turns out that the upward trend in income isn't matched by a corresponding uptrend in happiness. The fluctuations in income are occurring around a rising trend line and those in happiness, around a level trend line. The fluctuations in happiness and income—the short-run movements—are positively related, whereas the trends—the long-run tendencies—are not.

Grasping this distinction between the short- and long-run relationships—between the positive correlation of fluctuations and the nil association of trends—is crucial. Misunderstanding the happiness-income paradox, for example, a knowledgeable economist such as Diane Coyle writes, "The silliness of the notion that rising GDP does not increase happiness at all is even easier to see when you remember that a recession when GDP declines just a little makes people very unhappy" (Coyle 2014, 113). Here, Coyle is mistakenly citing the positive correlation between fluctuations in happiness and income to disprove the nil relation between trends. As we shall see later on (Chap. 14), this is a common mistake.

Another misconception is that the paradox says that, over the long run, happiness is constant. But the paradox is not about happiness alone; it is about the relationship of happiness to income. Countries can have rising, constant, or falling trends in happiness. *The paradox is this: There is no systematic correlation between the happiness trends and those in income.* Steeper uptrends in a country's income aren't accompanied by greater growth in happiness. The trends in China and Brazil provide an excellent example. Between 1990 and 2012, China had a much higher growth rate of real GDP per capita than Brazil, but Brazil's happiness trended upward, while China's trended downward.

3.2   Solving the Paradox

No one has a problem with the cross-section part of the paradox—that happiness and income go together. That's what everyone knows. It is the time-series piece—the nil relationship—that rubs us the wrong way. This is especially worrisome, because the time-series result is telling us what actually happens to happiness when people's incomes increase.

How could it be? The cross section says that more income causes greater happiness, but the time series shows no effect from higher income. Is one part of the paradox right and the other wrong? Could both parts be right? If so, how is that possible?

The answer is that both parts are right, and they can be reconciled via the concept of *social comparison*. To get at the nature of social comparison, let's start with a simple thought experiment: Imagine your income increases substantially, while the income of everyone you know stays the same. Would you be happier? The answer most people give, including the vast majority of students in every undergraduate happiness class that I've taught, is "yes."

But now let's reverse the question. Suppose your income stays the same, and everyone else's income increases substantially. What happens to your happiness? Most people, including again the majority of my undergraduates, say they'd be less happy. What others earn influences your satisfaction with how much you yourself make; in other words, you are engaging in *social comparison*, assessing your situation in light of others'. Wittingly or unwittingly, people compare themselves to others all the time.

Let's try another thought experiment, one that makes the effect of social comparison more explicit. But before we do, a step back, since I should clarify what I mean by the term "income": I mean income in *real* terms, what income will buy. Consider for a moment whether a household *money* income of, say, $30,000 per year is or is not a high income. The answer depends on how much $30,000 will buy. In 1950, when prices were less than one-tenth of what they are now, $30,000 was a high income—it could buy more than ten times what the same amount will buy today. Today, $30,000 is a low household income. According to the US Bureau of Labor Statistics, an income of $30,000 in 1950 put a household in the top 3% of households; in 2018, it places that income in the lower third. When I talk about comparing peoples' incomes or about changes in income, I will always mean *real* income—income after adjusting for any price differences. In other words, what income will buy.

Many economists and other analysts often use per capita Gross Domestic Product (or GDP, the economy's total output of goods and services) as an approximation to a country's average income per person because of the easy availability of GDP statistics. When I refer to per capita GDP here, I will always mean *real* GDP per capita, the country's average *quantity* of goods and services per person.

OK, sorry for the digression, but I've found from previous classes that it's necessary to avoid confusion about "income."

Now here's our next thought experiment:

1. Imagine you are just about to graduate and take your first job. Which would you prefer, A or B?

A) Earning $100,000 upon graduation.
B) Earning $50,000 upon graduation.

Easy choice. There is no doubt that here the A's have it.

2. But suppose instead the A and B options were as below. Which would you prefer, A or B?

A) Earning $100,000 upon graduation, when other graduates earn $200,000.
B) Earning $50,000 upon graduation, when other graduates earn $25,000.

Not so easy!

My guess is that you're hesitating. The $100,000 option now comes with the drawback that others will make twice that amount, while the $50,000 option reverses your comparative situation, giving you double what others earn. In fact, in my previous undergrad classes, about two-thirds of the students switch to option B. What others make plays a critical role in how satisfied they are with their own earnings. They prefer an income that is substantially more than that of others, even though it is smaller in absolute amount.

The key to all of this is a discovery some years ago by psychologists Daniel Kahneman and Amos Tversky (Fig. 3.2). They found that when people evaluate a particular circumstance, they typically have in mind a *reference level*, an

Fig. 3.2 Psychologists at ease: Amos Tversky and Daniel Kahneman (Courtesy of Barbara Tversky)

internal benchmark against which they judge the situation. In many cases, this reference level is established by social comparison, that is, observing the situation of others. For example, is a man of 5 ft 9 in. a *tall* man? The answer depends on one's reference level for height. In India, where the average height of men is 5 ft 6 in., he is likely to be considered tall. But in the United States, where the average height of men is 5 ft 10 in., he would not be so regarded. Americans' reference level for height is greater than Indians', because the "others"—the persons with whom their comparisons are being made—are persons who, on average, are considerably taller than those with whom Indians are making comparisons.

Similarly, how I feel about a given amount of personal income—whether it's a lot or a little—depends on how my income compares with others' incomes, that is, how it measures up relative to my reference level for income. In thought experiment one, which simply asks if I'd prefer a $50,000 or a $100,000 income, there is no mention of others' incomes. Implicitly, like respondents in general, I ignore others, assuming, in effect, no change in their incomes. Therefore, I judge that I'll be happier at A, where the absolute amount of my income is a lot greater than at B. But when it turns out that others' incomes are also increasing, as in question two, then I prefer the situation in which I have a lot more than others, option B, even though the absolute amount of my income is smaller than in option A. As in the height example, where a 5'9"American man is deemed short or tall by making a comparison with the height of American men generally, I judge whether my income is a lot or a little not by its absolute size but by how large it is compared with the incomes of others.

"So why do people think that more income will make them happier?" asks Lily, looking perplexed.

Well, Lily, is there a similarity between asking people if more income will make them happier and the first question in our thought experiment? In both cases people envisage a situation in which their income increases but that of others does not. In the real world, however, as the economy's total output increases, the incomes of most people generally move up more or less together. Hence, the *income reference level* (the incomes of others) rises along with one's own income, and the net effect on happiness of higher income is negligible. Everyone is experiencing a dual impact: the positive effect on happiness of an increase in his or her own income along with the negative effect of an increase in others' incomes. Of course, some people will have a greater increase in income than the average, and their happiness will increase. But if some people are moving up in the array of incomes, with their happiness increasing, others are necessarily falling behind, with happiness decreasing. The overall effect is no change in the average happiness of all persons taken together.

3.3   The Good Life: Wanting and Having

Answers to the *Good Life question*, included in intermittent annual surveys conducted by the Roper Organization since the mid-1970s, demonstrate how reference levels for evaluating income rise along with incomes. Each respondent is presented with a list and asked, "When you think of the good life—the life you'd like to have—which of the items on this list, if any, are part of the good life as far as you personally are concerned?" After the respondent has identified the items on the list viewed as comprising the good life—in effect, things they want—she or he is then asked to indicate "all the things [on the list] you now have." The answers thus give an idea of the things people *want* and the extent to which they *have* them. We can think of what they have as a reflection of how big their income is and what they want as an indication of their income reference level, the benchmark by which they are evaluating how much they have.

There are ten big-ticket consumer goods on the Good Life list, ranging from a home, car, and television set to travel abroad, a swimming pool, and a vacation home. (Take a look at the specific question and response items in Table 3.1.) Over time, as their income grows, people typically acquire more big-ticket consumer goods—in other words, they *have* more. But their survey answers show that the number of things they *want* also grows, and it grows to about the same extent as the number they have. A simplified example: All of the Johns have a car and TV at the time of college graduation, and within the next 5 years, they each add a home and second car to their possessions. The number of big-ticket items that they have thus grows, on average, by two. In the same period, however, the list of the good life items wanted by each also expands by two—let's say, to include a swimming pool and vacation home—so that the number of big-ticket items that they have and the number that they want both increase by the same amount. The fact that the number of goods wanted increases by the same amount as the number possessed signifies that the income reference level—the benchmark used in evaluating what one has—is rising right along with income.

What is the result?

In Ralph Waldo Emerson's eloquent words, "Want is a growing giant whom the coat of have was never large enough to cover."

Table 3.1 "Good Life" questions from Roper Surveys (Handout #3)

We often hear people talk about what they want out of life. Here are a number of different things

1. When you think of the good life—The life you'd like to have—Which of the things on this list, if any, are part of that good life as far as you personally are concerned?

Part of the
good life

Big-ticket items	A home you own
	A yard and lawn
	A car
	A second car
	A vacation home
	A swimming pool
	Travel abroad
	A color TV set
	A second color TV set
	Really nice clothes
Family	A happy marriage
	No children
	One child
	Two children
	Three children
	Four or more children
	A college education for my children
Health	Good health
Job	A job that is interesting
	A job that pays much more than the average
	A job that contributes to the welfare of society

2. Now would you go down that list and call off all the things you now have?

Now have

Big-ticket items	A home you own
	A yard and lawn
	A car
	A second car
	A vacation home
	A swimming pool
	Travel abroad
	A color TV set
	A second color TV set
	Really nice clothes
Family	A happy marriage
	No children
	One child
	Two children
	Three children

(continued)

Table 3.1 (continued)

We often hear people talk about what they want out of life. Here are a number of different things	
	Four or more children
	A college education for my children
Health	Good health
Job	A job that is interesting
	A job that pays much more than the average
	A job that contributes to the welfare of society

The shortfall of big-ticket items that people have compared with the number they want remains constant. In effect, incomes (what people have) and income reference levels (what people want) increase by the same amount, and the gap of unfulfilled wants remains the same. As incomes go up, happiness fails to increase, because income reference levels rise apace.

3.4   Social Comparison Revisited

"I don't know," Ted interjects. "I don't think my generation is that materialistic."

Maybe not, Ted, but social comparison is much more common than you think and doesn't apply only to income. It is a common feature of everyday life. Julia's pleasure in her A grade in statistics is suddenly reduced when she finds out that most of the class (her reference level) got A's. Matt's less proud of his time in the 100-yard dash when he learns it's typical of his age group (or cohort—his reference level). In many endeavors and situations, we are comparing ourselves to others, whether or not we are aware of it.

You may be sure that social comparison is at work everywhere. Not long after I published the Paradox article, I was having lunch with my colleague, the late Irving Kravis. He had just returned from Maoist China, where the leveling of social differences had reached the point of uniform dress in drab blue tunics. I asked him whether in such circumstances there was any indicator of status in people's attire. He replied immediately, "Oh yes, having a watch."

"Geez." Tyler shakes his head.

Geez is right. Despite a far-reaching effort, not even Mao could exterminate social comparison.

Previously, in the discussion of objective versus subjective measures of well-being, I noted that there may be a good psychological reason why happiness may not increase when incomes go up (Chap. 2). We now know what that reason is: *social comparison*. When others' incomes increase, everyone's income reference level rises, consequently undercutting the positive effect on happiness of an increase in one's own income.

Social comparison explains not only the negligible trend relationship between happiness and income but also the positive cross-section association. At a point in time, those with high incomes are happier than average, because most of the people with whom they compare themselves are worse off. Put differently, the income of the more affluent is above their income reference level. Conversely, those with low incomes tend to be less happy, because most of those with whom they compare themselves are doing better. The income of the less affluent is below their income reference level. Higher happiness goes with higher income, lower happiness, with lower income. At a point in time, happiness and income are positively related. This positive cross-section relationship—the rich being happier than the poor—turns up in the data year after year, since the same types of point-of-time comparison are continually being made by the rich, the poor, and everyone in between. Nevertheless, the long-run nil *time-series* relationship between happiness and income persists. For both higher- and lower-income persons, the positive impact on happiness of growth in one's own income from 1 year to the next is undermined by a corresponding growth in income of his or her income reference group.

Social comparison is a key to understanding the happiness-income paradox, explaining as it does *both* the cross-section *and* trend results. It may not be the whole story, but it is a major part of it. Moreover, social comparison provides a reason for the paradox, because it explains how there could be a nil time-series association, a positive cross-section relationship notwithstanding.

3.5 The Upshot

Jill still wants the answer.

"So, is increasing one's income a reliable recipe for raising happiness?"

No. If the aim is to increase happiness, you need a prescription that will work for everyone, or virtually everyone. Increasing income is not a reliable way to increase happiness, because if everyone increases his or her income, no one, on average, is happier. The increase in income reference levels as others' incomes rise undermines the positive effect of the increase in one's own income, and, on average, no one ends up better off.

The nil effect on happiness of more income illustrates what's called *the fallacy of composition*—namely, that what may be true for the individual is not necessarily true for the population as a whole. If I alone raise my voice in a restaurant, I will be heard better. What happens when everybody raises his voice? No one is heard better (though we might all get headaches). If I alone stand up at a football game, I have a great view of the field, but when everyone stands up, we all probably see worse than when we were sitting (and a likely altercation risks taking our attention from the game).

As a prescription for raising happiness, increasing income fits the fallacy of composition. If I alone increase my income, I will be happier. In contrast, when all people increase their incomes, no one, on average, is happier. As a way of increasing happiness, more income is what is called a *zero-sum game*—any gains in happiness by those whose incomes increase more than the average are offset by losses in happiness of those whose incomes grow less than the average.

"Wait!" Lily objects, "I thought it was *farewell* to the dismal science. This seems to be just the opposite."

True. What we need is a win-win recommendation—a way of increasing happiness that, if followed by each individual, would pay off for all, making everyone happier.

But let's not forget that there are important sources of happiness other than money, specifically the state of one's health and family circumstances—how do they impact happiness? Are there win-win solutions to matters of health and family?

Don't give up yet, Lily.

Because as we'll see, the answer is "yes."

References and Further Reading

Coyle, D. (2014). *GDP: A brief but affectionate history*. Princeton, NJ: Princeton University Press.

Easterlin, R. A. (1974). Does economic growth improve the human lot? Some empirical evidence. In M. Abramovitz, P. A. David, & M. W. Reder (Eds.), *Nations and households in economic growth: Essays in honor of Moses Abramovitz*. New York, NY: Academic Press.

Easterlin, R. A. (2010). *Happiness, growth, and the life cycle*. New York, NY: Oxford University Press.

Senik, C. (2009). Direct evidence on income comparisons and their welfare effects. *Journal of Economic Behavior and Organization, 72*(1), 408–424.

Thornton, A. (2005). *Reading history sideways: The fallacy and enduring impact of the developmental paradigm on family life.* Chicago, IL: University of Chicago Press.

Tversky, A., & Kahneman, D. (1991). Loss aversion in riskless choice: A reference-dependent model. *Quarterly Journal of Economics, 106*(4), 1039–1061.

4

How Does Health Affect Happiness?

4.1 Tracking Health and Happiness

"I do hope it's not more bad news today," mumbles Ted, as the class slowly settles down.

Well, let's see.

When people talk about what's important for their happiness, health is a leading concern. Cantril's survey questions about the best and worst of all possible worlds, for example, elicit responses like this: "I hope in the future I will not get any disease. Now I am coughing." Consistent with this, in the Good Life surveys of the previous chapter, virtually every respondent, young and old, cites good health as part of the Good Life, a key component of perfect happiness.

But does happiness change in response to ups and downs in health?

According to many psychologists, people adjust quickly and completely to a change in health—a development they term *adaptation*. In this view, people in short order get used to changes in their physical condition, so happiness is unaffected.

"Hard to believe," puts in Ted.

Perhaps, but as scholars, we want to put aside our beliefs and see, as we did with income, what the evidence has to say.

Cross-section evidence first.

Although over four decades old, an article by Philip Brickman and others is still the principal basis for the psychologists' claim that a person's health, good or bad, has little impact on happiness. This conclusion is due to the article's supposed evidence that people adapt quickly and completely to health

© The Author(s), under exclusive license to Springer Nature Switzerland AG 2021
R. A. Easterlin, *An Economist's Lessons on Happiness*,
https://doi.org/10.1007/978-3-030-61962-6_4

problems, even very severe ones, based on the finding that accident victims are no less happy than those who are accident-free. This is truly an astonishing result, because the accident victims in the article became paraplegics or quadriplegics as a result of their accidents. They were surveyed less than a year after their mishaps and were reportedly just as happy as their accident-free counterparts.

Despite its widespread acceptance by psychologists, there is much in this article that is problematic. The sample size is a questionable basis for safe statistical generalization: 29 accident victims are compared with 22 controls (respondents supposedly like the accident victims except that they have not had an accident). In my experience, to draw a reliable conclusion, samples of about 100 are usually needed.

This problem, however, pales in comparison with what one discovers from a careful reading of the text. The conclusion above, commonly reported in the psychological literature, is wrong. The Brickman et al. article states categorically that, compared with controls, the accident victims—paraplegics and quadriplegics—are significantly less happy. The common misreading results from the authors' subsequent assertion that the accident victims are not as unhappy as "might have been expected." But who is expecting what here? There is no way of knowing what "might have been expected"; this is a matter of imagination, or more precisely, an untold number of imaginations. The fact is that the study shows a demonstrably negative impact on happiness from a serious accident. In other words, insofar as the evidence in this article goes, happiness and health go up and down together. They are *positively* related.

There's much better and more comprehensive cross-section evidence on happiness and health. A little-known 1990 article by Thomas Mehnert and associates, published in a highly specialized journal, *Rehabilitation Psychology*, compares the life satisfaction of 675 persons reporting health problems with a nationally representative sample of more than 1,000 persons who do not have such problems. The health problems include physical disability, heart disease, respiratory disease, cancer, sensory conditions, and mental illness. The large sample size and coverage of persons with an assortment of health problems provides a more meaningful basis for generalization than the Brickman study of paraplegics and quadriplegics. Mehnert and his coauthors also include information on the severity of people's health problems, on whether respondents have more than one serious illness or disability, and on the extent to which the respondents are limited in performing daily activities, such as dressing or grooming.

The bottom line? People with health problems are significantly less satisfied with their lives than those who have no problems, a result consistent with the actual finding of the Brickman et al. article. Moreover, the gap in satisfaction between those with and those without problems is greatest if one's health problem is the most severe. For example, among those with no disability, 90 percent say they are somewhat or completely satisfied with their lives; by contrast, among those with very severe disability—and this would presumably include respondents akin to the paraplegics and quadriplegics of the Brickman study—the corresponding percentage is 49. Not surprisingly, the gap is also greater if people have two or more health problems or if their condition significantly hinders their ability to carry out daily activities.

In short, the evidence is that health problems decrease happiness, and the worse the problem, the greater the reduction in happiness.

Notably, both the Brickman and Mehnert articles are cross-section studies. The happiness-income paradox makes clear that cross-section findings are not necessarily a good guide to what actually happens over time. In the case of health and happiness, however, it turns out that the time-series pattern is consistent with the cross-section relationship.

A few years ago I assembled US data to trace what happens to physical health as cohorts age and, also, to see how satisfied they are with their health. As one would expect, physical health declines as people get older and does so fairly steadily. But what to predict about satisfaction with health? If people adapt quickly and completely to declining health, there should be no change in how they feel about their health. But, in fact, a decline in health satisfaction parallels that in people's actual health. In a nutshell, as people's health diminishes with age, so too does their satisfaction with their health, and, other things constant, declining satisfaction with health, in turn, reduces happiness. Thus, the evidence—both time series and cross section—is consistent. Health and happiness are positively related: they change together in the same direction.

4.2   Explaining Health and Happiness

Lily is at it again.

She raises her hand and asks, "But what about social comparison? Don't we have that here, too? My grandmother might think 'My health isn't as good as it used to be, but that's life. That's the way it is for old folks like me.' So, if that's the way she thinks, her satisfaction with her health would stay the same even though her actual health is getting worse."

Good thinking, Lily. Your example brings the reference level for health—the benchmark for evaluating health—directly into play along with a person's actual health. From what you hypothesize, your grandmother's benchmark for evaluating her health is the health of others her age. If, along with a worsening of your grandmother's health, her reference level for health declines equally because the health of her cohort is likewise deteriorating, then there would be no change in your grandmother's satisfaction with her health or with her happiness.

But what is our reference level for health? Is our benchmark analogous to that for income, the health of others?

Suppose instead your grandmother were to think, "I can't do many of the things I did when I was younger. I can't walk as fast or as far, sing as well, or play tennis anymore. My grandchildren are so cute, but I can't get down on the floor and play with them like I did with my own children in the past. I can only drive my car at certain times of the day and have to limit my reading because my eyesight isn't what it used to be."

Your grandma's standard in this case is her own past experience, not others her age, and when she was younger, she was much healthier and able to do many more things. When her reference level is her own past experience and her health worsens more and more with age, the shortfall of her health compared with her reference level increases. As a result, she is likely to become less and less satisfied with her health, and her happiness will decline.

So, which is it—in evaluating her health, is she comparing herself with her counterparts, or is she looking at her past experience? The evidence presented earlier that satisfaction with health trends downward with age along with actual health indicates that the reference level for health is based primarily on past experience, not comparison with others. If interpersonal comparison determined her reference level, her satisfaction with health would not decline as she got older, because on average, her peers experience the same deterioration.

Generally, two types of comparison affect reference levels: those with others and those with one's past experience. In other words, *inter*personal and *intra*personal comparison come into play as two different kinds of reference level. *Interpersonal comparison*, as we've already discussed, means social comparison, comparison with others (Chap. 3). *Intrapersonal comparison* is an evaluation by comparison with one's own personal best, as we might call it. For example, I play golf with a partner who had once been a scratch golfer, typically able to shoot a par score of 72. He is older now, invariably ends up scoring in the 80s, which makes him unhappy, because his reference level is his personal best. If his reference level had been my level of play (*inter*personal comparison), then he would be happier—indeed, he'd be flying to the moon. Alas, the 100 or more that I shoot is not even on his radar. Unfortunately for him, personal best (*intra*personal comparison) dominates his judgment.

In our analysis of happiness and income, *inter*personal or social comparison as the basis of an individual's reference level was in the forefront. People's material living conditions give us a good sense of their incomes, and these are readily perceived and learned by the rest of us. We observe, often quite closely, the kind of clothes other people wear, the number and make of the cars they drive, the sort of homes they live in, and the furnishings in these homes, perhaps even the vacation destinations they enjoy.

But income and health are two different things, especially in the degree to which they're perceptible to others. How much information do we really have about other people's health? A neighbor may mention a health problem from time to time, or you may observe her coughing or having difficulty walking. Yet when greeted with the customary "How are you?", most people mechanically reply "Fine." Conditions like heart disease, pulmonary disorder, or malignancy are seldom visible or widely advertised by the sufferer. Given the internal character of much illness and the lack of medical training among most people, our observations of others don't tell us much about their health. I had a colleague who recently died of brain cancer, but, sadly, I had no idea that he was sick, because he kept on teaching his classes almost to the very end. Illness is, at bottom, inherently personal in nature. Notice that one of the foremost concerns about Internet privacy is the possible disclosure of one's health records, an indication of how health tends to be highly confidential.

So, in determining reference levels for income and health, while interpersonal and intrapersonal comparison are both in play, their relative importance varies. *Inter*personal comparison dominates the reference level for evaluating an increase in income, and *intra*personal comparison is paramount in the reference level for assessing health. The difference is due to the comparative ease of obtaining information about other people's incomes versus the difficulty of knowing about their health. I have a good idea of my associates' incomes; I know very little about the actual state of their health.

In considering the effect on happiness of increasing income, we saw that because of interpersonal comparison, the reference level for income (the incomes of others) tends to increase along with one's actual income, and happiness remains unchanged. By contrast, when intrapersonal comparison chiefly determines the reference level, as it does for health, the happiness outcome is different. The reference level for health is rooted in past experience and usually changes much less than the reference level for income. Grandma evaluates her ability to do things today primarily in light of the many things she could do in the past, and that is a relatively fixed benchmark. If the reference level is pretty much constant, then happiness varies based on one's current situation, which means, in the case of health, better health raises happiness, and poorer health diminishes it.

4.3   Diagnosis

For health, in sum, both the cross-section and time-series evidence tell us that happiness rises and falls along with corresponding changes in one's actual health. One's current condition determines the effect of health on one's happiness.

"Well," remarks Ted in disgust, "There's not much we can do about getting older."

That's true but take it from me—getting old takes time. So, look at it this way: The positive association between health and happiness implies that improvements in health due, say, to diet and exercise will make you happier, whereas neglecting your physical condition is a prescription for unhappiness. The parallel movement of health and happiness emerges because our benchmark for evaluating for health is primarily past experience—pretty much our personal best—and this changes only to a limited degree as we progress through the life course. In contrast, the reference level for assessing our incomes is mostly determined by the current situation of others, so it changes in step with the increase of one's own income as the economy grows.

So, today we have good news, Ted. Unlike increasing your income, improving your health is a win-win situation. When everyone tries to increase his income, no one is happier, because reference levels increase along with income. Yet when all people exercise and improve their health, reference levels, grounded in the past personal experience of each individual, do not change, and everyone is happier.

So, for many of us, it's not that hard to keep smiling: go for that walk, avoid the fast-food chains, and get a regular check-up by your doctor. You'll be healthier and happier.

"O.K.—on my way to the gym now, professor!" Ted shouts, as he heads out the door.

References and Further Reading

Brickman, P., & Coates, D. (1978). Lottery winners and accident victims: Is happiness relative? *Journal of Personality and Social Psychology, 36,* 917–927.

Easterlin, R. A. (2015). Do people adapt to poorer health? Health and health satisfaction over the life cycle. In F. Maggino (Ed.), *A life devoted to quality of life: Festschrift in honor of Alex Michalos* (pp. 81–92). New York, NY: Springer.

Frederick, S., & Loewenstein, G. (1999). Hedonic adaptation. In D. Kahneman, E. Diener, & N. Schwarz (Eds.), *Well-being: The foundations of hedonic psychology* (pp. 302–329). New York: Russell Sage Foundation.

Mehnert, T., Krauss, H. H., Nadler, R., & Boyd, M. (1990). Correlates of life satisfaction in those with disabling conditions. *Rehabilitation Psychology, 35,* 3–17.

5

Family Life and Happiness

5.1   Making Matches

The class is all ears today—it's a topic of immediate interest: Does a partner increase one's happiness?

Not, I'm afraid, in the view of George Bernard Shaw: "There are two tragedies in life. One is to lose our heart's desire. The other is to gain it."

Shaw's witticism foreshadowed the perspective in psychology that we saw in the last chapter: People adapt quickly and completely to changes in their life circumstances, leaving happiness unaffected. In this view, even a sought-after soulmate is very soon yesterday's news.

Are Shaw and the psychologists right? Does finding a lifetime helpmate increase happiness, or do people quickly get used to having a partner, ending up no happier than before? And what about children—do they add to happiness?

Once again, let's look at the evidence, this time on family life and happiness. What do the data say?

Almost all cross-section studies report that those who are married are significantly happier than the unmarried. Consequently, researchers commonly conclude that marriage increases happiness. But is it *marriage* specifically that increases happiness, or is it that finding a lifetime partner does, whether the partners are married or not?

In fact, in the few cross-section studies that include those who are unmarried but cohabiting, it turns out that cohabiting and married persons are about equally happy. The evidence thus suggests that having a partner is what makes for greater happiness and that the marriage ceremony itself adds

R. A. Easterlin, *An Economist's Lessons on Happiness*,
https://doi.org/10.1007/978-3-030-61962-6_5

nothing more. However, most of the research on this subject studies partnerships formed through marriage, so that is why I mainly discuss marriage here.

The cross-section evidence that married persons are happier than unmarried seems to disprove the psychologists' view of rapid and complete adaptation to finding a partner. And yet, the psychologists not only disagree but offer a different interpretation of the evidence. In their view, the point-of-time difference in happiness between the married and unmarried does not demonstrate a causal effect of having a partner; it is due simply to what is called a *selection effect*. In this case, the selection is a result of personality characteristics—married persons, in their analysis, are characteristically more extroverted and less neurotic than unmarried.

Think of a representative sample of young people, say, those aged 18–25. There are significant personality differences among these young folks, as indexed by what psychologists call the Big Five measures of personality (extroversion, neuroticism, agreeableness, openness, and conscientiousness). So far as the effect on happiness of these characteristics is concerned, the evidence is that those who are extroverted and less neurotic are significantly happier. Extroversion and absence of neuroticism are also characteristics that are apt to attract a partner and lead to marriage. Psychologists, therefore, interpret the cross-section finding that married persons are happier than unmarried as an effect of personality—being extroverted and not neurotic—which makes individuals both happier and more likely to be married. According to their reasoning, those who are married are happier than others even before entering into a relationship, because of the selection effect due to their distinctive personality traits. The relationship itself does nothing to increase their happiness.

"Great," says Ted. "I guess my time is better spent at the gym."

Not only that, but a prize-winning 2003 coauthored article published in the *Journal of Personality and Social Psychology* presents time-series evidence supporting the conclusion that a partner has no effect on happiness. This study traces the happiness of a group of young Germans from 2 or more years before marriage (called the "baseline" period) to 2 or more years after marriage. An attractive feature of this study is that the same people are interviewed year after year in what's called a panel study, which enables assessment of whether the happiness of the same people after marriage is greater than their happiness in their baseline period, 2 or more years before marriage.

The authors find that the respondents' happiness, compared with the baseline value, goes up significantly a year *before* marriage—which they attribute to anticipation of getting married—and then has another statistically significant upward bump in the year of marriage. The study's principal finding, nonetheless, is that by 2 years after marriage, happiness has sunk back to its pre-marriage baseline level. The authors' explicit conclusion is that "[O]n average, people adapt quickly and completely to marriage."

Finding a partner has no enduring effect on happiness.

"Just great," says Ted again.

I can tell you that Ted isn't my only undergraduate who does not respond well to this article. Not surprising, considering that if we inspect the Good Life survey thoroughly, a happy marriage tops the list of things the students view as part of the good life. Fortunately for the students, though, I was able to counter the psychologists' study, thanks to the research of my then-graduate student, Anke Zimmermann Plagnol (Fig. 5.1). Anke re-ran the psychologists' analysis with more careful attention to control variables and found that, although there was some adaptation to marriage, it was significantly less than total. Her overall finding? Two or more years after marriage, the happiness of those who remained married was significantly higher than their before-marriage baseline value.

Take a look at Handout #4, Fig. 5.2, which sketches both Anke's findings on the course of happiness before and after marriage (labeled "ACTUAL") and the psychologists' (labeled "PSYCH"). Note that Anke's ending value of happiness is above the initial, or baseline, value, contrary to the psychologists' result, which ends back at the baseline. Anke's finding is that marriage has a significant positive impact on happiness, consistent with the positive relationship between marriage and happiness reported in cross-section studies, whereas the psychologists' result signifies no lasting effect.

Fig. 5.1 Anke with Timo and Delphine (Courtesy of Anke C. Plagnol)

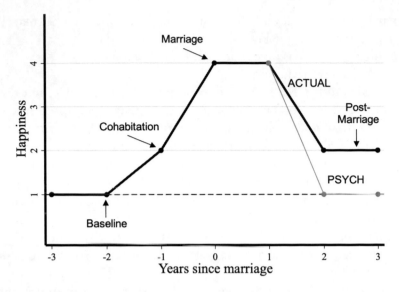

Fig. 5.2 Happiness before and after marriage (Handout #4)

Happiness increases in the year before marriage and again in the year of marriage. Happiness declines after marriage but remains above its baseline value (solid line), contrary to the psychologists' claim that it returns to the baseline value (light line).

Anke discovered, furthermore, that the increase in happiness observed in the year before marriage was due not to anticipation of marriage, as the psychologists assumed, but to cohabitation—that is, starting to live with one's prospective spouse. She also found that happiness 2 or more years after marriage, though significantly above the baseline value, was no different from the value in the year before marriage when cohabiting began (see Fig. 5.2). Her conclusion? *Forming a partnership, married or not, is what increases happiness*: marriage in itself has no additional effect—the same result as in the cross-section studies I noted at the start of this discussion.

For marriage, as in the case of health, the cross-section and time-series results agree.

As you might expect, my undergrads liked Anke's article best of all–better than any other on my lengthy reading list.

It makes sense that having a partner increases one's happiness. We are, after all, social animals. Normally, partners provide emotional support, sexual intimacy, and companionship. And loneliness is the common complaint of single persons. There are, of course, exceptions, but as they say, exceptions prove the rule.

"Now you're talking! Headed to the gym and then the juice bar."
And it looks like a number of other students are following Ted's lead.

5.2   Breaking Up: Hard to Do?

It is hardly news that many unions break up. The estimate is that in the United States, 40 to 50 percent of first marriages will end in divorce. Does divorce make people happier? And what about widowhood—what's the impact on the happiness of the surviving partner, or when a new partnership is formed following a break-up? Is happiness as great the second time around?

As we've seen, the cross-section evidence is that those not in unions are significantly less happy than those who are. However, in these studies, the happiness of those not in unions varies depending on the reason for their single state. The happiness shortfall is least for persons who never had a partner or who are widowed. It is significantly greater for those who are divorced, and the unhappiest group of all is persons who are separated—that is, in a transient state, still married but no longer living together. According to the cross-section data, nonetheless, there is hope for those in broken marriages, since those who remarry are just as happy as those still in their first marriage.

Time-series studies of broken relationships are scarce, but the fragmentary evidence for divorce and widowhood are consistent with these cross-section results. In her analysis, Anke looked at those in her sample who ended up divorcing, and she found that they were significantly less happy after divorcing than in their baseline period before marrying. Thus, both cross-section and time-series evidence say that divorce does not make people happier, though divorced persons may be better off than those who are separated.

The psychologists' study looked at widowhood, and the results chimed with those in cross-section data. Widows were significantly below their baseline value of happiness.

Note that the psychologists' result for widowhood contradicts their previous finding that marriage does not increase happiness and further calls into question the marriage results. If forming a union doesn't increase happiness, why should losing a partner reduce it? In contrast, Anke found a symmetrical relationship: Happiness increases when one has a partner and decreases on losing one. And cross-section data support this symmetry.

5.3   The Patter of Little Feet

According to the Good Life surveys, most people want children. Similarly, a large majority of students in my classes look forward to having children. Yet whether children actually increase happiness over the life course is unclear.

Once again, I draw on the research of a former graduate student, this time Maggie Switek (Fig. 5.3). Using detailed panel data collected by Swedish demographer Eva Bernhardt, Maggie was able to trace the happiness of several birth cohorts of women and men in Sweden as they progressed through the first 20 years of adulthood, up to age 40. She found that, in the year before childbirth and for 2 years thereafter, the happiness of women increases, but after that, children start making mothers less happy. Men's happiness changes in the same ways as women's, but the size of the changes is too small to be

Fig. 5.3   Maggie (Courtesy of Maggie Switek)

significant. The gender difference in the impact of children on happiness is probably the result of a difference in values. Many women find parenting more important than a job outside the home, while for men, the opposite is true.

Not surprisingly, the class is displeased with the negative turn in happiness due to children, which runs counter to their belief that children consistently contribute to greater happiness.

"Are you saying I'd be happier as a stay-at-home mom, Prof. Easterlin?" asks Jill.

No, Jill—we're not headed in that direction. But there is a good explanation for the ambivalent or even negative impact of children on happiness, an explanation that goes beyond the so-called terrible twos. Think of children's effect on happiness as the outcome of two components—satisfaction with family life, which is initially increased by the presence of a child, and satisfaction with finances, which is decreased by the expense of childcare and child-rearing. During pregnancy and children's infancy, satisfaction with family life has the upper hand, and happiness increases. Pretty quickly, though, the financial strains of raising children overshadow the family-life effect. Thus, when parents of children 2 or more years of age are asked, "How satisfied are you with your financial situation?", the answers, compared with what went before, are significantly negative. In the course of time, satisfaction with family life tends to diminish, too, because of difficulties of combining work and parenting as well as the emergence of concerns about teenage problems like possible drug use and similar peer pressures.

5.4   Assessing Family Life

This time I'm ahead of Lily! ... But now Andy's taking her place.

"What about reference levels for family life? Don't they play a part for happiness and family? Looking at who's got a partner and who doesn't, comparing them ... I bet there's plenty of interpersonal comparison there."

Then you'll be a bit surprised, Andy—because the answer is that reference levels for family life, like that for health, are fairly fixed, depending more on intra- than interpersonal comparison. This is obviously so in the case of marriage. According to the Good Life survey, almost everyone at all ages wants a happy marriage, so there's little change in marriage aspirations over the life course. Most strikingly, even many women over 45 years of age who have never married express this desire. Although their prospects of actually finding a spouse are low, a majority continue to cite "a happy marriage" as part of the good life as far as they *personally* are concerned. You might suppose that, having been single well into middle age, these women would have adapted to that state, thinking that to be free and on one's own is the good life. But more than half still want a happy marriage, which suggests that, even for persons with a strong incentive to change, the reference levels for family life—in this case, a happy marriage—remain pretty stable. The failure of those who never married to achieve a happy marriage doubtlessly helps explain why, on average, they are significantly less happy than those who married.

Additionally, as is true of health, social comparison doesn't much affect reference levels for family life, since it's likewise difficult to know the situation of others. How much do we really know about the family life of our associates anyway—how well a couple is getting along with each other and with their children? How often have we been surprised to learn that what we thought was an ideal couple is breaking up? Speaking personally, I don't even know for sure how my grown children's marriages are faring. We have considerably fewer clues as to the family lives of our relatives and associates than we do as to their financial situation. The benchmarks for evaluating family life are based much more on each person's own past experience than social comparison.

That family life goals are basically fixed is true not only for marriage but also for offspring. Economists distinguish between the number of children that parents want, the desired *quantity* of children, and parents' preferences regarding things like the health and education of the children, termed child *quality*. The Good Life survey indicates that desires regarding both quantity and quality don't change much over the parents' life course. Irrespective of what is happening to others, the number or *quantity* of children a couple wants remains generally constant. When they married, Fred and Clarissa wanted two children; their good friends, Peter and Agnes, wanted three. Once each couple reaches its desired family size, they are content. Social comparison doesn't come into play: Fred and Clarissa are happy with two children, even though Peter and Agnes have three. In contrast, when Peter and Agnes modernize their kitchen with an island, granite countertops, and oak cabinets, Fred's and Clarissa's kitchen now looks to them like a scullery. Linoleum flooring! Alas, in spite of the fact that neither cooks, they've raised their standard for evaluating their material circumstances—their income reference level—and they are less satisfied than before with their home.

Similarly, goals for the health and education of one's children, their *quality*, also don't alter much over the life course. Not surprisingly, people always want their children to have good health. But this might surprise you: There's also little change in the proportions of parents wanting college versus high school educations for their children, even though incomes, on average, are growing.

Peter and Agnes may be making more money, but they continue to be satisfied if their children can complete high school. So says the survey evidence.

"Maybe," interjects Lily, glancing over toward Andy. "But don't parents compete to send their children to the 'best' schools? That's interpersonal comparison."

Surely, from early on, many parents are trying to get their children into what they believe are the best schools. But in what way and to what extent do parents compete over the education of their children, Lily? Specifically, does social comparison lead to an *escalation* of education goals? That's the issue here. Peter and Agnes' kitchen remodel, on one hand, leads Fred and Clarissa to set a new standard: Their own kitchen will be the center of the party, with catered brie en croute, roasted vegetables, and French wines artistically displayed on the new island's granite countertop. On the other hand, they don't raise goals for their own children's education based on what happens to Peter and Agnes's children. Although social comparison may lead to greater spending to achieve people's educational aspirations for their children—for example, by hiring a private tutor or, as we've recently learned through the media, by bribing admissions personnel at elite schools—schooling objectives, by and large, remain fixed.

5.5 The Bottom Line

"So, family life's like health?" asks Ted. "An easy way to happiness?"

Spot on! We can all increase our happiness by bettering our family life and health. If I improve my family life by spending more time with my spouse and kids, my behavior doesn't affect anyone else, because the reference levels of those folks, like mine, are based on their own past experience. As a result, my family (including me) is happier, and so are all others who do the same. It's simple: This route to happiness is available to all. And if hiking or biking is part of our family time, then, the family earns a health dividend that further boosts happiness.

The outcome? Increased happiness of all: a win-win situation.

References and Further Reading

Crimmins, E. M., Easterlin, R. A., & Saito, Y. (1991). Preference changes among American youth: Family, work, and goods aspirations, 1976–1986. *Population and Development Review, 17*(1), 115–133.

Lucas, R. E., Clark, A. E., Georgellis, Y., & Diener, E. (2003). Reexamining adaptation and the setpoint model of happiness: Reactions to changes in marital status. *Journal of Personality and Social Psychology, 84*, 529–539.

Plagnol, A. Z., & Easterlin, R. A. (2008). Aspirations, attainments, and satisfaction: Life cycle differences between American men and women. *Journal of Happiness Studies, 9*, 601–619.

Switek, M., & Easterlin, R. A. (2018). Life transitions and life satisfaction during young adulthood. *Journal of Happiness Studies, 19*, 297–314.

Waite, L. J., & Luo, Y. (2009). Marital happiness and marital stability: Consequences for psychological well-being. *Social Science Research, 38*(1), 201–212.

Zimmermann, A. C., & Easterlin, R. A. (2006). Happily ever after? Cohabitation, marriage, divorce, and happiness in Germany. *Population and Development Review, 32*, 511–538.

6

How Can I Increase My Happiness?

6.1 Having Vs. Wanting

"OK," says Ted, dejectedly. "I didn't think this would be so hard." He's still got his headphones in, and it looks like he's ready to leave. "So, I'm really glad to see the topic of today's class, professor. Just tell us. *How can I increase my happiness?*"

Yes! We're ready for the big question.

Let's bring together our results so far, putting things in basic terms, like "Have" and "Want." "Have" indicates your *actual circumstances*, and "Want" characterizes *reference levels*, the internal benchmarks we use in evaluating circumstances (although we often do so pretty much unbeknownst to ourselves). Take a simple example: Tim, who is 7 years old, has one Slinky, but he wants four. The shortfall of the amount needed to make him perfectly happy is three.

Generally, happiness increases the more you have and the less you want. If your wants are constant, your happiness grows as what you have increases. But if what you have remains the same, and wants increase, happiness shrinks. So, if Tim's stock of Slinkys grows from one to two, while the number he wants remains at four, the shortfall declines to two, and he's happier. But if Tim's stock of Slinkys stays at one, while the number he wants increases from four to five, his shortfall rises to four, and he's even less happy.

If what you want and what you have both increase equally, happiness is unchanged. Tim's stock of Slinkys increases from one to two, while the number he wants goes from four to five. His shortfall remains the same at three, and he is neither more nor less happy.

© The Author(s), under exclusive license to Springer Nature Switzerland AG 2021
R. A. Easterlin, *An Economist's Lessons on Happiness*,
https://doi.org/10.1007/978-3-030-61962-6_6

There's not much new about this. Two and a half centuries ago, Samuel Johnson put it this way: "Every man is rich or poor according to the proportion between his desires and his enjoyments; any enlargement of wishes is therefore equally destructive to happiness [as] the diminution of possessions" (Johnson 1751, 242).

Back to the adult world. Personal happiness depends basically on three circumstances: economic situation, family life, and health. What you want—the benchmark used in evaluating what you have—depends, in general, on two things, comparison with the circumstances of others (interpersonal or social comparison) and comparison with past experience (intrapersonal comparison). The vast majority of people engage in interpersonal comparison to evaluate their economic situation yet employ intrapersonal comparison to assess health and family life. Interpersonal comparison is more important in evaluating one's economic situation than in assessing health and family life, because the situation of others is much more easily determined from everyday observation of their lifestyle than is their health or family life.

If I make more money and my economic situation gets better, what I Want tends to grow to the same extent as what I have. The growth in what I want occurs because the incomes of others rise in step with the growth of my own income and, via social comparison, raise my income reference level, the benchmark for judging whether my own income is satisfactory. So, with what I want increasing to the same extent as what I have, my happiness stays the same as my income grows.

For health and family life, however, what I Want does not change with what I Have. Why? The benchmarks we apply to health and family life are grounded in past experience and change little. In consequence, if my health or family life improve, that is, what I Have gets better, my happiness increases, because what I Want doesn't change.

6.2   What Can I Do to Increase My Happiness?

"Hey! I have a good idea," says Emma, jumping in for the first time. "We—," she glances behind her, "I mean, Ted—should stop making interpersonal comparisons."

The whole class laughs.

"That way, he won't want more stuff he doesn't need and be less happy just because other people have more stuff."

Good reasoning, Emma—if at Ted's expense!

Too many people end up buying a house larger than they need and a deluxe car (or cars) to display their wealth. The result is to burden themselves, with colossal debt and the stress of meeting large debt repayments month after month. It's awfully hard to enjoy your BMW if you can barely afford the gas to drive it.

Because income trends upward during the working ages, you might think that people would become increasingly satisfied with their financial situation. Yet, in fact, there is very little change in financial satisfaction throughout the prime working years, due to the burden of debt repayment brought about by perpetually multiplying the list of things we want. It's not until folks are into their retirement years, with incomes leveling off or even declining, that financial satisfaction improves noticeably. Children have completed school and are mainly self-supporting. Material aspirations decline as needs diminish in the so-called golden years, and the burden of debt is substantially reduced as mortgages and other debts are finally repaid.

The lesson?

"We can all increase happiness by focusing on what we really need and not worry about keeping up with our neighbors!" Ted exclaims.

Yes, Ted, good on you and Emma: We can increase happiness by addressing our true needs and avoiding unnecessary debt.

A pretty easy lesson? Sure, yet a word of warning: Eliminating social comparison is easier said than done. I live, for example, in quite a nice house. Some time ago, my daughter Molly's soccer coach invited us to his residence for a get-together of players and parents (Fig. 6.1). His house turned out to be quite grand, and I must admit that when I got back to my own dwelling, my pleasure in it was somewhat diminished.

As Karl Marx says, "A house may be large or small; as long as the neighboring houses are likewise small it satisfies all social requirement for a residence. But let there arise next to the little house a palace, and the little house shrinks to a hut" (Marx, 1847, 163).

I should know better than to indulge in social comparison, but it's hard to break the habit. Nevertheless, it's definitely worth the effort. (Note to self: Remember this!)

There's a second, and perhaps easier, route to increasing happiness: improving our use of time. Each of us has only a given amount of time, and the more we devote to one activity, say, making money, the less time there is for others, like improving health and family life. Because wants regarding health and family life are relatively fixed compared with wants for living conditions, devoting time to an improvement in one's health or family life will have a more lasting effect on happiness than increasing one's income.

Fig. 6.1 Molly at soccer (Courtesy of Molly C. Easterlin)

Unfortunately, people spend a disproportionate amount of time trying to make more money, at the same time shortchanging things like family life and health. Look at the responses to this survey question: "Imagine you are 38 years old and offered a new position in a field you like. The job is more prestigious and will pay 15 percent more than your present job. It will also require more work hours and take you far away from your family more often. What is the likelihood you would take the job?" (Glenn 1996, 26).

There are four response options. About a third of respondents say it is "very likely" that they would take the job; another third say "somewhat likely," and the remaining third say "somewhat unlikely." *Not one person chooses the fourth option, "very unlikely."* Thus, in a survey in which respondents had previously said "having a happy marriage" was their top life goal, family life is sacrificed to make more money. What's more, in all likelihood, health would suffer because of longer work hours and more time on the road. The preference for the new job option highlights how people typically misallocate time by down-playing family life and health relative to making money.

It's probable that some respondents who choose the money option rationalize their decision on the grounds that, despite their absence from home, more money will make for a happier family life—that money will substitute for personal presence. OK, but what sorts of things make people happy? In fact, many of the things that people enjoy, that make them most happy, require little or no money, though they do require time. Over the past few decades, numerous studies reveal how people use their time. People's responses, based on personal diaries, cover the usual range of daily activities. Fortunately, one nationally representative inquiry hit on the idea of also asking respondents how enjoyable each activity was. The answers are on a 10-point scale from 1 (=dislike) to 10 (=like). Here are the most enjoyable activities (a rating greater than 7.5) ordered from high to low in terms of average score:

9.3 Sex	8.5 Church, sleep, attend movies
9.2 Play sports	8.3 Read book, walk
9.1 Fishing	8.2 Relax, magazines, visit, work break, meals away
9.0 Art, music	8.0 Talk with family, listen to stereo
8.9 Bars, lounges	7.9 Lunch break
8.8 Play with kids, hug and kiss	7.8 Home meal, TV, read paper
8.6 Talk to kids, read to kids	7.7 Knit, sew

What stands out is that most of these activities don't cost a lot, and some require no money at all. However, they do require time. Taking a job that would "require more work hours and take you far away from your family more often" would leave much less time for many of these sources of happiness.

This survey of enjoyable activities is over 30 years old, so some items such as "knit" and "sew" seem out of date, at least for a large portion of the population. Perhaps now "surfing the Internet" and "tweeting" might substitute for knitting and sewing. Nonetheless, the essential findings of this early study are largely confirmed by a somewhat similar collaborative study, published in 2004 by psychologist Daniel Kahneman (again! the reference-level pioneer) and others. Those surveyed were Texas women who worked the previous day and were easy to reach, a convenience rather than random sample. The three items leading the list of most enjoyable activities are "intimate relations," "socializing," and "relaxing." All three fit well with the items above. They take time, certainly, but they require little or no money.

"So why do people do this—use up their time trying to make money?" asks Lily, looking perplexed.

Exactly so, Lily—why do we? Very often, people misallocate their time, choosing the pursuit of money at the expense of other life goals. Why?

"Because they think a lot of money will make them happy," blurts out Ted.

Yes, that's the answer: because of the common belief that more money makes you happier. People don't realize that their material wants increase in step with what they have. The expected increase in happiness resulting from more money turns out to be illusory, while the loss of happiness due to the sacrifice of family life and health is real.

So, what will make you happier? Despite what I felt after leaving the soccer coach's house, I know the answer is "more time devoted to things like family life and health, less time to the pursuit of money."

Focus on soccer, not the coach's house.

References and Further Reading

Easterlin, R. A. (2003). Explaining happiness. *Proceedings of the National Academy of Sciences, 100*, 11176–11183.

Easterlin, R. A. (2006). Building a better theory of well-being. In L. Bruni & P. L. Porta (Eds.), *Economics and happiness: Framing the analysis* (pp. 29–64). New York, NY: Oxford University Press.

Glenn, N. D. (1996). Values, attitudes, and the state of American marriage. In D. Popenoe, J. B. Elshtain, & D. Blankenhorn (Eds.), *Promises to keep: Decline and renewal of marriage in America* (pp. 15–33). Lanhman, MD: Rowman and Littlefield.

Johnson, S. (1751). *The Rambler.* No. 163 (October 8). https://en.wikiquote.org/wiki/SamuelJohnson

Kahneman, D., Krueger, A. B., Schkade, D. A., Schwarz, N., & Stone, A. A. (2004). A survey method for characterizsing daily life experience: The day reconstruction method. *Science, 306*(5702), 1776–1780.

Marx, K. (1847). Wage labor and capital. In *Marx-Engels Selected Works*, I, p. 163.

Plagnol, A. C. (2011). Financial satisfaction over the life course: The influence of assets and liabilities. *Journal of Economic Psychology, 32*(1), 45–64.

Robinson, J. P., & Godbey, G. (1997). *Time for life: The surprising ways Americans use their time* (2nd ed.). University Park, PA: Pennsylvania State University Press.

Part II

Next Lessons

7

Can Government Increase My Happiness: Transition Countries

7.1 East Germany: The Eye-Opener

Back in class, I have at least one anxious-looking student.

"Excuse me, professor," says Zack, looking perturbed, "But before you start—one of the guys that I know who took this class before said that this next class is about how great socialism is."

"Well, Zack, that's not exactly where we're going today. The central question is this: 'Can the government increase happiness?' And I have to tell you, the answer is an emphatic 'yes' whether the government is socialist or capitalist."

Public policy counts and—brace yourself—welfare-state policies especially boost happiness. Now before you conclude that, yes, I am a godforsaken socialist, let me say that this is not at all where I started. Nor does it mean that you have to be a socialist to favor welfare-state policies. I was forced gradually to recognize the positive impact of welfare-state policies on happiness by the accumulating evidence. As Senator Elizabeth Warren puts it, explaining her reversal on the causes of household bankruptcy, "I did the research, and the data just took me to a totally different place."

So, come along and follow the path of my enlightenment. In this class, I'll recount the first stage of the journey, my schooling in the transition from socialism to capitalism in Eastern Europe and China.

My education started with socialist East Germany. The question: Did happiness there increase after unifying with West Germany in October 1990? Along with most Western economists, I expected that because of the transition from socialism to free market capitalism, the answer would be an easy "yes."

But the data told a different story. To my surprise, 25 years after the start of the transition, the period spanned by the data, happiness was little better than that recorded in a June 1990 survey, taken when East Germany was still a socialist state. Happiness declined abruptly from 1990 to 1991 as unification occurred and, over the next two and a half decades, slowly recovered to about where it was just before the transition to capitalism began.

Tyler's hand shoots up.

"But East Germany was a police state. Do you think that we can trust a survey done by that government? Maybe before unification, people were afraid, so they gave exaggerated responses, saying how happy they were?"

A good, tough question from Tyler. The somewhat surprising answer is that the survey responses do seem trustworthy. There are two pieces of evidence supporting this view. First, there are so-called "domain" satisfaction questions in the surveys that ask about satisfaction with specific aspects of one's life, such as satisfaction with income, with health, and with family life. In the 1990 survey of pre-unification East Germany, all three of these domains get an average value of six or more on a scale of 0–10. But responses to questions about satisfaction with the environment and with the availability of goods are conspicuously worse. On each of these issues, East German respondents give an exceptionally low rating, little more than three. Scores in the neighborhood of three are very rare in European surveys of people's satisfaction, whatever the domain. But in this case, the low scores are consistent with the comments of foreign visitors to East Germany, who frequently complained about the air pollution and the absence of goods on stores' shelves (Fig. 7.1). The agreement of East German survey responses with visitors' observations on the sorry state of both the environment and availability of goods strongly indicates that East Germans were reporting how they really felt. In short, if they were candid about air quality and scarce goods, deficiencies for which the government could easily be held responsible, why would they falsify their answers on things like income, health, and family life?

Second, according to research by economist Timur Kuran, it wasn't uncommon for people in Soviet-style police states to express publicly feelings of discontent with their personal circumstances. Examining several of these countries before their transition to capitalism, Kuran found that newspapers received letters of complaint in abundance, especially regarding economic conditions. *Preference falsification*, a concept devised by Kuran to express the difference between one's private and publicly stated views, did occur, but it was limited almost entirely to political matters. Apparently, expressing

Fig. 7.1 East Germany's air pollution (Credit: Peter Jordan/Alamy Stock Photos)

dissatisfaction with other conditions of life, such as the environment and availability of goods, was permissible, and people took advantage of the opportunity.

Thus, the 1990 life satisfaction responses in socialist East Germany appear credible. But if this is so, then we're left with an even more difficult question.

"Yeah," agrees Jill. "How could that be?!"

Sure, Jill—that's exactly what I wanted to know: How could overall life satisfaction under socialism possibly be greater than under capitalism?

To solve this puzzle, I had to dig deeper into pre- and post-transition conditions in East Germany.

The collapse of life satisfaction from 1990 to 1991 accompanies a precipitous decline in output, amounting to about one-third of GDP. The flip side of the decline in output is a massive increase in unemployment as numerous firms go bankrupt.

In country after country, unemployment reduces happiness substantially— so says the evidence. Not surprised? But wait: This documented decrease in happiness occurs not only for the unemployed but also the employed, whose fear of job loss increases. Consistent with this, as unemployment in East Germany became epidemic, life satisfaction plummeted. The sharp decline was, however, short-lived, because West Germany stepped in and buffered the failing East German economy with a substantial income support program. Life satisfaction turned slowly upward.

Exacerbating the economic collapse, a second factor, dissolution of the social safety net, further reduced happiness. Again, the domain satisfaction data are illuminating. Satisfaction with health care, childcare, and work were all surveyed from 1990 onward, and all decline noticeably in the transition to capitalism. Under socialism, jobs were assured, and most men and women of working age were in the labor force. Unemployment was virtually nonexistent. Employers provided childcare and financed comprehensive health care. With the transition to capitalist free markets, the guaranteed job that existed under socialism vanished, and satisfaction with work consequently declined. So too did satisfaction with health care and childcare, perks of employment that disappeared as firms shifted from public to private ownership. It was the end of what some writers referred to disparagingly as the "socialist greenhouse." Those writers may not have liked the greenhouse, but to judge from the domain satisfaction responses, it looks like many of the public did. Satisfaction with childcare, health care, and work were all much higher under socialism than subsequently.

If the numbers here aren't enough for a convincing picture, qualitative accounts of the effects of the transition on people's lives provide additional support for the quantitative evidence of the initial plunge in life satisfaction. Here's a description by British labor market analyst Roger Lumley contrasting pre- and post-unification conditions:

> Over the 40 years of its existence the DDR [East Germany] had developed as a completely different state from the BRD [West Germany]. There was no unemployment, no (open) inflation, low work intensity, free medical and social services, low prices for housing and public transport…. Less than one year after unification, a sense of disillusion, disadvantage and insecurity was being felt by many in the East. Some looked back to the DDR as a golden age where everything was simpler, the food tasted better, and people were members of the community. (Lumley 1995, 29–30)

As illustration, Lumley quotes a 1991 East German survey respondent:

> The unification process is costing me personally DM400 each month. I include in this higher rental and transport costs, as well as social costs. There are problems at all levels: traffic, crime, prices, rent, refugees, health care, social security. For me personally it is a vast and serious problem. People have lost old structures and certainties, and don't know how to cope. I know that we here in the

East have to go through a transition process, but it is difficult and for many no longer makes sense.

This personal testimony gives life to the economic statistics. The 1990–1991 collapse of happiness in East Germany reflected the emergence of pressing new concerns about jobs, family, and health due to the abrupt contraction of the economy, soaring unemployment, and the breakdown of the social safety net. West Germany moved quickly on the policy front to forestall further deterioration, and alongside a gradual improvement in the underlying economic and social conditions, satisfaction with life gradually recovered.

Tyler quietly absorbs the evidence. But now Keaton has a question.

"OK, but let's go back to the political situation. What about the changes there? East Germany was also transitioning from an authoritarian police state to democracy. Wouldn't that increase happiness?"

Good thinking. But let's recall the results of Hadley Cantril's surveys of people's hopes and fears in 13 countries worldwide (Chap. 2). Whatever the political environment, when you ask people about the things important for their happiness, they mostly cite their immediate personal circumstances— making a living, raising and caring for a family, and ensuring good health. For the most part, these are the things that occupy their day-to-day lives and that they think they can do something about. Only around 1 person in 25 mentions broad systemic issues such as the form of government or political and civil rights.

How might Cantril's findings illuminate the results of the East German survey? Although unification meant that the average East German had new political freedoms, any positive impact of this on personal happiness was far outweighed by new worries about things closer to home, like finding a job, supporting a family, and dealing with health problems.

South Africa's transition to democracy highlights how personal concerns eclipse the political situation in people's life-satisfaction feelings. When the African National Congress took control of the government in 1994, there was a short-lived spike in happiness, but 1 year later, with conditions otherwise no better, happiness was back to its pre-democracy level. The transition to democracy failed to provide a lasting bump in happiness.

Pre-transition conditions in East Germany show that, to increase citizens' happiness, policies promoting full employment and a strong social safety net do the job. Contrary to what I'd expected, happiness under socialism was, on average, fairly high. While I'd previously been thinking that institutional change—the transition from a planned economy to free markets—would increase happiness, the research on East Germany's transition, in keeping with

Cantril's surveys, revealed the paramount nature of immediate personal concerns about making a living and caring for everyday family and health problems. Under socialism, government policy takes care of these cradle-to-grave issues, whereas under capitalism, they have frequently been left to be sorted out by the free market.

7.2   The Former Soviet Union: More of the Same?

My class isn't easy to convince, however.

"But is there a pattern?" Sue wants to know. "Maybe other countries aren't like East Germany. You know, they were unifying with West Germany. Did happiness change like East Germany's in other Eastern European countries that were shifting from socialism to capitalism?"

Because life-satisfaction statistics under socialism are hard to come by, Sue's question is not easy to answer. Fortunately, though, data are available for five members of the former Soviet Union: Belarus, the Russian Federation (hereafter Russia), and the three Baltic states. For each country, there are three life-satisfaction observations spanning the 1990s—the first in 1990, on the eve of the transition; the second, around mid-decade; and the third, at the end of the decade. Life-satisfaction statistics for Hungary are also available, but since they lack a mid-decade observation, they can't show us what happened in the course of the decade.

All five countries with mid-decade observations turn out to have transition patterns much like East Germany's. Over the decade of the 1990s, GDP declines abruptly and then starts to recover, a pattern roughly replicated by the intermittent statistics for life satisfaction. Changes in both unemployment and the social safety net are like those in East Germany—a severe worsening and then gradual improvement. An expert comment on pre-transition Russia even echoes that quoted earlier on East Germany:

> Before 1989, Russians lived in a country that provided economic security: unemployment was virtually unknown, persons were guaranteed and provided a standard of living perceived to be adequate, and microeconomic stability did not much affect the average citizen. (Brainerd and Cutler 2005, 125)

Indeed, the life-satisfaction data for 1990, around the start of the transition, probably understate the levels that had prevailed under socialism. In two countries, Russia and Hungary, for which 1980s data exist, life satisfaction is significantly higher in the years before 1990.

It's no exaggeration to say that the economic collapse at the onset of the transition devastated family life everywhere. The disintegration of the customary system left many families in turmoil as they tried to cope with family responsibilities while job opportunities and social support were disappearing. Some families moved back to villages in proximity to urban centers, attempting thereby to couple subsistence agriculture with nonfarm employment. Symptoms of social stress grew dramatically. Alcoholism, smoking, and drug use increased, especially among men, and suicide rates surged. Along with these came a rise in violence against women as well as increased divorce. The fabric of normal life was totally destroyed. All of this confirms and underscores the substantial declines reported in life satisfaction. As we might predict from Cantril's surveys, happiness dropped as family life suffered enormously.

Before looking at East Germany, I, like many Western economists, had paid little attention to what was happening to the 400 million people of Eastern Europe, assuming that with the transition to capitalism, everyone would be vastly happier. I couldn't have been more wrong. It's no exaggeration to say that the catastrophe there was comparable to the suffering in the capitalist countries of the West during the Great Depression of the 1930s. In the United States, unemployment soared to an unprecedented level; when the Depression hit rock bottom, one out of every four workers was out of a job. People lost their life savings and their homes, ending up on the street, in breadlines, and in soup kitchens. Shantytowns like today's homeless encampments sprang up everywhere (Fig. 7.2). Many suffered severe mental distress, and family life was shattered. So, to comprehend what has happened in Eastern Europe, we need look no further than the West's Great Depression.

The enormous human costs of economic failure are much the same everywhere.

Over the past two decades, happiness in most Eastern European countries has been trending gradually upward, but in most countries, it's likely still short of where it had been a decade or so prior to the transition. This long and difficult period has been a substantial part of many people's lives.

7.3   China Clinches It

"So, does a poor country like China follow the European pattern?" demands Sue. "Are you saying that it's the same everywhere, professor?"

Fig. 7.2 US shantytown, 1930s (Credit: World History Archive/Alamy Stock Photos)

A murmur goes through the class, because that's what they all want to know: Are these examples globally representative?

The question's more than fair, and, to be honest, I didn't think we'd see a global pattern. China's GDP trajectory was much more favorable than Europe's: vigorously upward, not collapsing. Between 1990 and 2015, GDP increased in China at the fastest rate ever recorded anywhere, doubling and redoubling. By the end of the period, most urban households had a color TV, an air conditioner, a washing machine, a refrigerator, and a personal computer. Because China's pre-transition living level had been so low—in 1990, GDP per capita was less than 10% of that in the United States—it seemed incredible that during the transition, life satisfaction worsened.

But it did. Life satisfaction went down significantly from 1990 to around 2002. Thereafter, it increased but in 2015 was still below its 1990 value. To my surprise, China turned out to have a U-shaped movement in life satisfaction, much like that of the Eastern European countries. Five different Chinese surveys came together to reveal this pattern. Once again, my expectations were wrong.

"I don't understand. How could people be less happy when per capita GDP increased like that?" Jill asks, echoing my initial puzzlement. "Doesn't getting all that stuff you mentioned show that people are much better off?"

Yes, Jill, that was my question, too: Don't all those numerous big-ticket consumer goods, including many very useful ones, make people happier?

As before, I tell my class that to solve the puzzle, I needed to delve into the underlying conditions. When I did, I discovered, much to my surprise, that in 1990, prior to the transition, the life satisfaction of urban workers in China was high. Not only that: Two China specialists linked the high pre-transition life satisfaction explicitly to the existence of a "mini-welfare state":

> Until recently, job rights have … been firmly entrenched in urban China.… State-owned enterprises have … supplied extensive welfare benefits, including housing, medical care, pensions, childcare, and jobs for [grown] children.… Almost all state employees, and many in the larger collectives, have thus enjoyed an "iron rice bowl" … lifetime tenure of their job and a relatively high wage in the enterprise representing a "mini welfare state." (Knight and Song, 2005, 16–17)

Thus, while from an international perspective 1990 material living levels in China were low, for a population raised under and accustomed to such conditions, these "mini welfare state" arrangements relieved concerns about work, family, and health, and they led, therefore, to substantial satisfaction with life. Indeed, a contented urban population was seemingly the government's implicit policy objective. In effect, there was a Faustian bargain, according to which potential popular discontent in the cities was bought off in return for the assurance of an "iron rice bowl," the good life as perceived by most Chinese at that time.

But in the early 1990s, to stimulate economic growth, China's leaders embarked on a policy of economic restructuring, initiating a move toward partial privatization of the economy. The policy was officially described as "grasping the big, letting go of the small." You can understand what this means if you picture an array of thousands of firms, ranging from a small number of high-productivity big firms at the top down to a very large number of low-productivity small firms at the bottom. The small number of high-productivity big firms accounts for much of the output, but the large number of low-productivity small firms employs by far the most people. In essence, the government "grasped" the big firms and "let go" of the small ones by shifting to the large firms the resources it had been using to keep the small firms going. It poured into the big firms not only financial resources but also the best human talent available, both white and blue collar.

The new policy was highly successful—for output growth. Because of the redistribution of major government support to the high-productivity large firms, GDP went up at an unprecedented rate. But the labor market was a different story—in fact, a human disaster. Thousands of small firms previously dependent on government subsidies went bankrupt, and massive unemployment ensued, hence, the seeming contradiction of rapidly rising GDP (the achievement of the large firms) and falling employment (the result of numerous small firms, the major employers, failing).

In my preconceptions, I'd been misled by that favorite measure of economists: GDP. But people aren't dollars or numbers, and what I learned is that *jobs, not GDP, matter for happiness.*

A recent paper by David Blanchflower and Andrew Oswald on mental distress in the American population brings home the critical importance of jobs. Since 1993 the proportion of the population saying, in effect, that "every day of my life is a bad day" has risen noticeably, most of all among less-educated midlife white men and women, among whom more than one in ten identify with this statement. Why? The principal reason, according to the statistical evidence is "I am unable to work," due to a marked decline in the availability of manufacturing jobs.

And there's more than that to the lesson of China. In addition to lost jobs, the social safety net previously enjoyed by the urban population was in tatters, due largely to deliberate government policy. Gone was the iron rice bowl: guaranteed lifetime employment and attendant cradle-to-grave perks. Unemployment benefits were available to only a very small proportion of those who lost jobs, and as the government privatized the health-care system, a rising number of people couldn't afford treatment. So, too, retirement pension coverage declined sharply.

In China, as in Europe, the brunt of economic restructuring fell on workers, and particularly the most disadvantaged segments of the working population, those with less education than others and with low incomes. Added to this, the floating population of China, migrants from rural areas to the cities, suffered severely. The better educated and more affluent, in contrast, were usually able to maintain old jobs or find new work, and their life satisfaction changed relatively little. But life satisfaction of the bulk of the population, which had previously been quite close to that of the more affluent, declined noticeably. Concerned and anxious about finding work, dealing with illness and accidental injury, caring for children and elders, and ensuring prospects for one's children, their happiness hit the skids.

In the early 2000s, faced with extensive and rising unemployment, China's government shifted gears and began to modify the policies of the 1990s. Employment rates gradually improved, but they remained well short of the previous full employment level. The government also took steps to patch the social safety net, introducing new measures to improve health care and pensions. The result? A modest recovery in reported life satisfaction, the upside of the "U"—though even by 2015, the level was still below the pre-transition value.

Keaton's hand shoots up.

"But you said China's living conditions improved a lot. Wouldn't that make people much happier?"

Ah … but social comparison is doing its dirty work, undermining the positive effect of material gains on happiness. This habit of glancing to the yard next door isn't lost on a number of native Chinese researchers, who note the prevalence of social comparison in China, or "keeping up with the Wangs." But the surge in benchmark incomes is perhaps best captured by the tongue-in-cheek conclusion of a novel by one of China's most popular and widely read authors, Zhang Bing. The central character, a government bureaucrat, is showing his fiancée the new apartment he has purchased for them:

He: "This is our little nest. We will spend 100,000 yuan to renovate it properly."

She: "We should buy a full set of home appliances, a VCD player, a 29-inch television set, an automatic washing machine, an air-conditioner, and a complete set of wooden floors."

And so the door to happiness opened.

This disillusioned voice issues from a country where 25 years earlier per capita income was less than one-tenth of that in the United States.

And there it is. Wants increase along with Haves.

References and Further Reading

Blanchflower, D. J., & Oswald, A. J. (2020). Trends in extreme distress in the United States, 1993–2019. *American Journal of Public Health*. Published online ahead of print, Aug 20, 2020.

Brainerd, E., & Cutler, D. (2005). Autopsy on an empire: Understanding mortality in Russia and the former Soviet Union. *Journal of Economic Perspectives, 19*(1), 107–130.

DiTella, R., MacCulloch, R. J., & Oswald, A. (2001). Preferences over inflation and unemployment: Evidence from surveys of happiness. *American Economic Review, 91*(1), 335–341.

Easterlin, R. A. (2009). Lost in transition: Life satisfaction on the road to capitalism. *Journal of Economic Behavior and Organization, 71*(1), 131–145.

Easterlin, R. A. (2012). Life satisfaction of rich and poor under socialism and capitalism. *International Journal of Happiness and Development, 1*(1), 112–126.

Easterlin, R. A. (2014). Life satisfaction in the transition from socialism to capitalism. In A. Clark & C. Senik (Eds.), *Happiness and economic growth: Lessons from developing countries* (pp. 6–31). Oxford, UK: Oxford University Press.

Easterlin, R. A., & Zimmermann, A. C. (2008). Life satisfaction and economic conditions in East and West Germany pre- and post-unification. *Journal of Economic Behavior and Organization, 68*(3), 433–444.

Easterlin, R. A., Wang, F., & Wang, S. (2017). Growth and happiness in China, 1990–2015. In J. F. Helliwell, R. Layard, & J. D. Sachs (Eds.), *World happiness report 2017* (pp. 48–83). New York, NY: Sustainable Development Solutions Network.

Knight, J., & Song, L. (2005). *Towards a labor market in China.* Oxford, UK: Oxford University Press.

Kuran, T. (1991). Now out of never: The element of surprise in the East European revolution of 1989. *World Politics, 44*(1), 7–48.

Lumley, R. (1995). Labor markets and employment relations in transition in countries of central and eastern Europe. *Employee Relations, 17*(1), 24–37.

Moller, V. (2007). Researching quality of life in a developing country: Lessons from the South Africa case. In I. Gough & J. A. McGregor (Eds.), *Well-being in developing countries: From theory to research* (pp. 242–258). Cambridge, UK: Cambridge University Press.

8

Can Government Increase My Happiness: Nordic Countries

8.1 Happy Welfare States?

So far, we've looked at countries transitioning out of socialism, and in these countries the time-series evidence is essentially the same in country after country. Under socialism, jobs were certain, and an extensive social safety net prevailed. Personal concerns about work and income security, family, and health care were largely satisfied. Happiness was high, mainly because the less advantaged segments of the population were just about as happy as those who were better off. With the transition to free markets, job certainty disappeared, and the safety net was in tatters. The less advantaged were especially hard hit. As policies assuring jobs and benefits vanished, a flood of new worries and anxieties about everyday life emerged, and happiness plunged.

The experience of the transition countries demonstrates that for people's happiness, employment and safety net policies are of vital importance.

"That's all great for them," says Ryder, "but would the policies that increased happiness under socialism work in capitalist countries? Can you prove that?"

An excellent question, Ryder, so let's see what the evidence tells us. Since the things affecting personal happiness are the same in capitalist and socialist countries, the answer is presumably "yes." To see whether this is right, let's take a look at what are widely recognized as the quintessential welfare states, Norway, Sweden, Denmark, and Finland—collectively, the Nordic countries. They were among the leaders in introducing employment and social safety net legislation toward the end of the nineteenth century and in building on this foundation throughout much of the twentieth. Today, the safety net spending of these countries as a percentage of GDP is about the highest in the world.

© The Author(s), under exclusive license to Springer Nature Switzerland AG 2021
R. A. Easterlin, *An Economist's Lessons on Happiness*,
https://doi.org/10.1007/978-3-030-61962-6_8

Although time-series statistics on happiness do not go back far enough to determine how the introduction of welfare state policies influenced happiness, in recent cross-section surveys, these countries consistently turn up as the world leaders in happiness, suggesting that welfare state policies and happiness go together.

"Yes," says Ryder, "but the Nordic countries have high incomes. Maybe it's not the policies that make people happier, but their incomes?"

Well, we've already seen considerable evidence that increasing income does not increase happiness—the United States (Chap. 3) and China (Chap. 7), for instance. So, let's take a closer look at the evidence for the Nordic countries. Although we do not have the time-series data that we'd like, we can see how happiness in the Nordic countries compares with that in countries that have the same income as the Nordic group but less generous safety net policies. Doing so enables us to rule out income (approximated by GDP per capita) as the source of any difference in happiness between the Nordic countries and their comparison counterparts and to see if policy differences may influence happiness.

In this comparison, our first group—let's call it the "ultra" welfare group—is the Nordic countries of Denmark, Sweden, and Finland. I'm omitting Norway, because its income is noticeably higher than those in the other three. The second group includes four semi-welfare states, the United Kingdom, France, Germany, and Austria, which I've selected because their average GDP per capita in the survey year 2007 is basically identical to that of the ultra-welfare group. The average unemployment and inflation rates in the two groups are also alike. Thus, overall economic conditions, not just GDP per capita, are approximately the same in the two groups. Yet benefit generosity, which includes how easily a person qualifies for benefits, how long they last, and how close they come to replacing wages, is much higher in the ultra-welfare group.

Can you guess? The ultra-group, the one with more generous benefits, turns out to be significantly happier than the semi-group.

My students are still skeptical.

"But couldn't the countries in the ultra-group be happier for another reason?" Ryder asks. "O.K.—forget about economic conditions. What about something like lower crime? Or more fresh fish and stronger beer?" (Classmates giggle.) "Seriously, though—are you sure it's benefit generosity that causes greater happiness in that group? Do people really notice these things? And even if they do, how do we know it makes them happier?"

Ryder's right: Although we've ruled out differences in GDP per capita as a possible cause of the greater happiness of the ultra-group, we can't safely conclude that the ultra-group is happier simply because it has more generous benefit policies.

Trying to eliminate explanations other than benefit generosity would be a never-ending job—so, doubtlessly, there is still some room for uncertainty. But with the help of unusually rich survey data, we can strengthen the case for a causal link between happiness and benefit generosity. Thanks to questions rarely asked in surveys, it's possible to establish that people in the ultra-group are both aware of the more generous policies they enjoy and feel good about them. Thus, evaluating the quality of public services in five areas—health, education, childcare, care of the elderly, and pensions—respondents' in the ultra-group rank their services significantly higher than those in the semi-group *on every single item.* People in the Nordic group *know* that their public services are good.

What's more, the ratings of these public services are reflected in people's satisfaction in the domains associated with these services. The ultra-group's satisfaction levels are significantly higher than the levels of those in the semi-group for health, family life, and work. Better health services reduce health concerns, better public child and elderly care reduces family worries, and so on. The survey results not only show peoples' awareness of the vital support that safety net policies in their countries provide but also reveal their happiness with these more generous policies. More beneficent policies underlie the greater happiness of the ultra-group.

So, then, what does the evidence suggest?

Ryder raises his hand and then stands.

"I think you'd put it like this: Under capitalism, government can improve people's well-being with the kinds of policies that prevailed under socialism."

The class laughs.

And how right he is!

Moreover, it's the less advantaged who particularly enjoy improved well-being when benefits are more generous, just as is true under socialism. In both the ultra- and semi-groups that we've just been looking at, the life satisfaction of the more affluent is about the same, but that of the less advantaged is much higher in the ultra-group.

8.2   Some Welfare State FAQs

"Yeah, but Sweden has a really high suicide rate," Emma persists. "Why is that—if welfare state policies have made Sweden one of the happiest countries in the world?"

In fact, the widely held belief that suicide is high in Sweden is untrue. The fact is that Sweden and the Nordic countries overall don't have high suicide rates. In 2015, Sweden ranked 68th on the male suicide rate out of 183 countries worldwide; Denmark was 106th and Norway 111th. Finland at 37th was the highest of the Nordic countries. (We'll see shortly why it's an outlier among the Nordic group.) In case you're wondering about the United States, its suicide rate is about the same as Finland's.

If we compare the Nordic countries with other European countries only, male suicide rates in all of the Nordic nations are below the European average, except for Finland. I use the suicide rate for men, because almost everywhere in the world, men's rate is several times higher than that for women and exceeds the rate for both genders combined.

Emma's question assumes that happiness and suicide are inversely related—that low happiness leads to a high suicide rate. While intuitively most of us might expect this to be the case, in fact, happiness and suicide don't correlate, either worldwide or in Europe. So, what is the overriding determinant of suicide rates? The volume of alcohol consumed, especially distilled spirits. Worldwide data are available for the last 40 years, and countries in the so-called vodka belt—mostly the Eastern European transition countries—are among those with the highest suicide rates in the world, while Islamic countries, where drinking intoxicants is for the most part forbidden, are among the lowest. In the 1990s, Sweden was part of the vodka belt and had a considerably higher suicide rate than at present. It is possible that the data for this earlier period are the source of the current belief that suicide is high in Sweden. Subsequently, a very high tax rate on distilled spirits shifted Sweden's alcohol consumption away from distilled spirits to beer and wine, and the suicide rate declined noticeably. Among the Nordic countries, only Finland still consumes a high proportion of hard liquor, and, as we've seen, its suicide rate is the highest of the Nordic group.

If alcohol consumption as a cause of happiness differences is set aside, which we can do by only looking at countries with similar alcohol consumption levels, higher suicide is weakly related to lower happiness. Nevertheless, this relationship is barely significant and applies only to data for all countries worldwide. It doesn't hold for regional groupings like Europe or Latin

America. In short, there is no strong evidence that low happiness is itself an important cause of suicide.

But my students haven't exhausted their questions.

"Yes, but the generous benefits in the welfare states reduce the work ethic. Right?" Owen asks. "And this reduces economic growth, right?"

Again, some analysts (and many politicians) insist that this is the case. Like the belief that suicide is high in Sweden, the notion that social benefits undermine a nation's work ethic is commonplace. Yet, how does it hold up against the evidence? If true, we'd expect to find fewer people working in the Nordic countries. To the contrary, the proportion of employed working-age persons is typically high in the Nordic states, higher than in both the United States and the average of the European Union countries. In the past half-century, moreover, the growth rate of real GDP per capita in the Nordic states has, on average, exceeded that in both the United States and European Union. Thus, the evidence doesn't show that welfare state policies have had an adverse impact on people's willingness to work and, more generally, on the rate of economic growth.

Lily's been listening to this debate between her classmates and me, but she's still not convinced.

"What about taxes in the Nordic states? Aren't they really high?"

Taxes are, indeed, considerably higher than in countries with a less extensive and less generous social safety net. The OECD puts the ratio of government tax revenue to GDP for the Nordic countries at 53%; this compares with a European Union average of 45 and a US value of 33. And yet the people in the Nordic countries are willing to pay high taxes. Why? Because the tax revenue mostly goes to paying for programs that alleviate pressing personal concerns. For example, job security is a constant worry in many countries—these days, many people fear that employment opportunities will be lost as robotics take over the assembly line. But Sweden, an ultra-welfare state, doesn't express this fear. A 2017 *New York Times* article on worker attitudes toward a robotic future reports that Swedish workers aren't worried about losing jobs due to technological advances. According to a survey by the European Commission, "eighty percent of Swedes express positive views about robots and artificial intelligence..." By contrast, a survey by the [United States] Pew Research Center found that "72% of Americans were 'worried' about a future in which robots and computers substitute for humans."

Why are the Swedes less concerned about robotics? The answer is simple. As the *Times* article shows, quoting the Swedish minister for employment and integration, "The jobs disappear, and then we train people for new jobs. We won't protect jobs. But we will protect workers."

And the Swedes know this.

8.3   Are Welfare State Policies a Luxury of the Rich?

"Like you said, people in the Nordic countries have high incomes," Emma counters.

"Aren't most countries in the world too poor to provide the safety net policies you're talking about?"

Actually, it's the other way around—in most nations, incomes are currently high enough to support welfare state policies. Denmark was a leader in introducing such policies back in the 1880s, when its per capita GDP, expressed in today's prices, was just over $3000. Currently, three-fourths of the population of the less developed world lives in countries with a GDP per capita equal to or greater than that amount, so welfare state policies are within reach in much of the world.

Costa Rica is a case in point, demonstrating that less affluent countries can implement and maintain such policies. Costa Rica started welfare state programs in the middle of the twentieth century when its GDP per capita was about the same as Denmark's in the 1880s. Today, it is one of the happiest countries in the world, ranking 13th out of 156 countries. By comparison, the United States, whose per capita GDP is four times that of Costa Rica, ranks 18th. Surely, Costa Rica's policies account for its high level of happiness.

So, it's something of an illusion to think that economic growth, which raises people's incomes, undergirds welfare state policies. Economic growth can make it easier to pursue such policies, but it's not essential. For happiness to increase, what is needed is a government in place willing to use tax revenues to carry out safety net policies. Quite simply, these policies can be implemented in the absence of economic growth.

8.4   The Upshot

So, that's it.

The historical record points consistently to the positive relation between welfare state policies and happiness. In nations transitioning from socialism to capitalism, happiness plummeted as governments abandoned welfare state policies. In the Nordic countries, which have led the pack in the introduction of welfare state policies, happiness is the highest in the world.

Two disparate types of evidence, then, dovetail nicely: on the one hand, Cantril's findings that, when it comes to their happiness, people are most concerned about their economic situation, family, and health and, on the other, consistent evidence that welfare state policies focusing on these areas raise well-being. Can government increase people's happiness?

The answer's a flat-out "yes."

At the same time, there's no single optimal menu of welfare state programs. For a range of reasons, the specifics differ considerably among countries and are constantly being re-examined and revised. But the broad outlines of government policies that will increase happiness are pretty clear. The list includes full employment and income support programs; available housing; universal health care; schooling, childcare, and parental leave programs from pre-K through higher education; and old-age social security—in short, an iron rice bowl for all.

And, a final cautionary note. Government policies, on one hand, and the political and economic systems under which policies are implemented, on the other, are two different things. In this and my earlier discussion (Chap. 7), I neither make claims about nor present evidence for the superiority of any given political or economic system. So let's lay to rest Zack's earlier fear that I'm campaigning for radical political change. My interest is in happiness. According to the evidence, happiness can be fairly high in socialist societies and under authoritarian regimes. But this hardly means that socialism is preferable to capitalism or police states to democracy. As the Nordic countries show, happiness can be, in fact, quite high in democratic and capitalist societies. The bottom line is that *specific policies* are important for happiness, and these policies may be carried out under different types of political and economic regimes.

8.5 Consumer Sovereignty and the Welfare State

Some economists are advocates of *consumer sovereignty*, the belief that consumers' choices should govern what goods are produced, and the government's functions should be minimal. According to this view, individuals are the best judges of their own interests and should be able to spend their money as they wish, free from government taxes or regulation, as long as they do no harm to others. Government intervention in spending decisions is dismissed as paternalism, derided as "Daddy knows best!"

The findings of happiness research call into question the doctrine of consumer sovereignty, because they show that people aren't infallible when it comes to assessing their best interests. Households err systematically in their decisions about the effect of increasing income on happiness. The choices people make under the presumption that more money will increase happiness fail to do so, because people's income reference levels—ignored in economics and by advocates of consumer sovereignty—increase and alter the expected outcome. If people aren't always correct in judging their own interests, then, as the evidence we've seen suggests, government can adopt policies that will increase their happiness.

However, economists, especially in the United States, are loathe to depart from the doctrine of consumer sovereignty. Thus, in a perceptive article depicting multiple ways in which the free market falls short of optimal outcomes, two Nobel prize-winning scholars end with this caution: "The fact that people sometimes fail to maximize utility does *not* imply that someone else … should usurp the right to choose." They opt for what has come to be called "nudging," a procedure by which "those 'in charge' … guide and influence choices without restricting anyone's freedom to choose" (Kahneman and Thaler 2006, 231–232).

The nudging approach has its merits, but the reluctance to opt explicitly for government policy intervention betrays a woeful misunderstanding of the history of social progress. Economic theory and economic history shape the worldview of many economists in the United States, and these subdisciplines extol the benefits of free markets and focus solely on economic experience. But viewing the world through an economic lens leads to a distorted perception of social progress and its sources. Since the mid-nineteenth century, life expectancy at birth has doubled just about everywhere in the world. This enormous advance in the human condition is the result, not of the free market or economic growth, but of the development of biomedical knowledge that spurred the establishment, most notably, of public health systems. Often, these systems recommend and employ compulsory policies and procedures like quarantine and mandated vaccinations that have done much to raise life expectancy.

As I write, we are in the midst of the first phase of a coronavirus pandemic. No one expects a free market binge or polite nudge to stop the spread of this disease or to limit the number of deaths. Strong and rapid governmental intervention is required; consumer sovereignty—aka panic buying—is an obstacle, not a help. All of the bleach and toilet paper in the world can't begin to match the benefits of officially sanctioned shelter-in-place, face masks, and social distancing requirements when it comes to a deadly disease for which to date there's no vaccine or antibody test.

Much the same is true of establishing a welfare state: consumer freedom to spend as one wishes will not do it, nor will "nudging." "Consumer sovereignty" has an appealing ring to it, but the truth is that it is basically a call to minimize taxation. In fact, as we have seen in this discussion, the happiest countries are the Nordic countries whose rank in taxes as a percent of GDP is among the highest in the world. As the actions of the democratically elected governments of these countries demonstrate, taxation with a view to bettering human well-being is a proven way of improving individual happiness, though it runs directly counter to consumer sovereignty.

References and Further Reading

Easterlin, R. A. (2004). How beneficent is the market? A look at the modern history of mortality. In R. A. Easterlin (Ed.), *The reluctant economist: Perspectives on economics, economic history, and demography* (pp. 101–140). Cambridge, UK: Cambridge University Press.

Easterlin, R. A. (2012). Happiness, growth, and public policy. *Economic Inquiry, 51*(1), 1–15.

Friedman, J., & McCabe, A. (1996). Preferences or happiness? Tibor Scitovsky's psychology of human needs. *Critical Review, 10*(4), 471–480.

Kahneman, D., & Thaler, R. H. (2006). Utility maximization and experienced utility. *Journal of Economic Perspectives, 20*(1), 221–234.

9

Happiness or GDP?

9.1 Happiness Vs. GDP

"OK," says Dan, "Maybe government policies can increase happiness, but why should the government care? Shouldn't it be focusing on economic growth—on GDP—not happiness?"

It's true that, for over half a century, GDP per capita has been the principal measure of well-being and that increasing GDP has been a dominant goal of policy-makers. But prioritizing GDP puts businesses in the forefront along with policies focused on increasing output, whereas happiness centers on human beings and leads to programs that improve people's everyday lives.

China, where GDP and happiness moved in opposite directions in the 1990s, highlights the merits of happiness versus GDP as a summary measure of well-being and a guide to policy. As you know, in the years after 1990, China's GDP increased at perhaps the highest rate ever documented, a feat acclaimed by numerous observers as the "China Miracle." At the same time, however, happiness went down. Which measure, happiness or GDP, better captures the change in people's well-being?

The answer? "Happiness," certainly. China's policy of economic restructuring, though it raised markedly the growth rate of GDP, involved major collateral damage, including, most importantly, massive unemployment and dissolution of the social safety net. The result, for those still employed as well as the unemployed, was new and pressing worries about jobs and income security, family life, and health. No wonder that social policy analyst Gerard Lemos declares that "the Chinese people are deeply insecure about themselves and their future" (Lemos 2012, 3). In promoting the expansion of output,

© The Author(s), under exclusive license to Springer Nature Switzerland AG 2021
R. A. Easterlin, *An Economist's Lessons on Happiness*,
https://doi.org/10.1007/978-3-030-61962-6_9

policy-makers totally neglected what was happening to the workers. Yet if they'd been guided by happiness, they would have seen how disruptive the new policies were to the lives of the Chinese people. China's happiness decline underscores the serious human costs of putting output before people.

A recent event in the United States and the government's response to it offers yet another example of how focus on GDP leads to minimizing people's lives. A 35-day partial shutdown of the US government starting in December 2018 led to the layoff of hundreds of thousands of federal government employees and federal contract workers. Commenting on reports of the stress and suffering felt by these workers, Secretary of Commerce Wilbur Ross responded:

> Put it in perspective. You're talking about 800,000 workers. And while I feel sorry for the individuals that have hardship cases, even if all those workers were never paid again, you're talking about a third of a per cent of our GDP, so it's not like it's a gigantic number overall.

Here we have GDP weighed directly against the lives of hundreds of thousands of workers, and GDP wins out. To Secretary Ross, who views things from a GDP perspective, the suffering of nearly a million workers is insignificant, because their lost income (and output) amounts to a tiny fraction of GDP. Not to put too fine a point on it: If GDP is so little affected, what happens to people really doesn't matter! To say the least, this is a striking illustration of how putting output first can lead to downright inhumanity, intended or not.

In contrast, a focus on happiness puts human beings first.

Why else prefer happiness to GDP? Happiness is a much more comprehensive measure than GDP. Calculated on a per capita basis, GDP approximates at best people's average real income—that is, the average quantity of goods and services produced and, for the most part, consumed by the members of society. Happiness, conversely, registers the effect on well-being of not only income but also developments in other important aspects of people's lives. These include, most centrally, their job situation, health, and family circumstances. Happiness assessments therefore encompass the many concerns of everyday existence, whereas GDP is simply about income.

And surely, happiness is a measure with which people can personally identify, unlike GDP. The man sitting on the couch watching the news sees "GDP Up by Five Per Cent," yawns, and quickly turns to ESPN. But when the commentator proclaims, "Happiness Up by Five Per Cent," he tunes in. People understand and care about happiness; GDP is mostly a remote and mysterious concept.

Furthermore, in measuring happiness, the individuals whose well-being is being assessed render the judgment, not outsiders. By contrast, so-called experts, the statisticians who put the numbers together, calculate GDP, not those to whom the numbers presumably refer.

Moreover, happiness is a measure in which each adult has a vote, but only one vote, whether rich or poor. In contrast, the choices of the affluent, who have more purchasing power, disproportionately determine what goods are produced and make up the content of GDP.

"But happiness just depends on people's perceptions. It's subjective," protests Dan. "Isn't GDP preferable because it's a hard number?"

"Yes! I was thinking the same thing, professor—GDP statistics are hard facts," chimes in Zack.

Dan and Zack echo the preconceptions of many economists, who think of GDP as a "hard" statistic, somehow equivalent to a materially observable output, like say, that of iron ore. In contrast, many economists view survey statistics reflecting people's views and feelings as "soft" data. This may seem like a plausible dichotomy, but as we'll see down the road, the distinction between soft and hard, objective and subjective, and quantitative and qualitative is a hangover from the twentieth-century behaviorist era of economics, when it was an article of faith that what people said was not to be trusted (Chap. 15).

Truth be told, there is no single hard figure for GDP. In measuring it, numerous subjective judgments about what to include are required, as Nobel Laureate Simon Kuznets, the pioneer in GDP measurement, repeatedly pointed out. Should unpaid homemakers' services like caring for children, preparing meals, and housecleaning be included in GDP? They're not, yet when the same services are performed by hired employees, they are. How about food produced by farm families for their own consumption? Included, though the same families' preparation of this food for their meals is not. Prostitution, gambling, alcoholic beverages, and narcotics: in or out? This depends mainly on the legal status of these products and pursuits, which differs among and within countries and changes over time (witness the Prohibition Era). What about defense spending—are Americans better off by the amount of their country's huge military outlays, which are included in GDP, than Costa Ricans, who do not even have a standing army? Questions like these about what to include must be faced in constructing an estimate of GDP. GDP is thus by no means a hard, objective measure: The subjective judgments of those who put the numbers together determine what constitutes GDP.

"Wow," says Lily, "I had no idea."

But this isn't to say, Lily, that we should throw GDP away. If you want to know specifically about the economy's output, GDP is a useful tool. By the same token, if you want a summary measure of health, life expectancy is a reasonable gauge. But if you want a comprehensive measure of people's overall well-being and a clear-cut guide to policy, then happiness is the answer. Happiness embodies what really matters in people's lives. It directly reflects the principal circumstances of ordinary people everywhere in the world.

Some scholars object to the idea of happiness as an official metric of well-being, claiming that people might falsify their reported happiness. Others complain that the measure gives too little importance to systemic considerations like political and civil rights. These are plausible concerns, but their proponents offer no alternative summary measure of well-being, leaving us where we are now, with GDP. Happiness may not be the last word in determining well-being, but it's better than GDP.

Others criticize happiness measures because they have, unlike GDP, an upper bound—that is, a specific limit. As currently measured, the highest happiness can go, whether for an individual or country, is a value of 10. In contrast, GDP can just keep going up and up. It is, at least theoretically, limitless.

This is a curious complaint. Is it better to have no upper bound? The view that there should be no upper bound implies that society's goal should be unattainable—for example, that we can never have enough output—and that it would be unfortunate if we were ever to reach an upper bound. This way of looking at things is a sure road to dissatisfaction. Alfred, Lord Tennyson put it this way: "All experience is an arch wherethrough/Gleams that untraveled world whose margin fades/Forever and forever when I move." Romantic yearnings only get you so far, as happiness disappears over the horizon.

A more meaningful perspective, perhaps, envisions utopia as a society where each person reports the upper bound, a maximum happiness value of 10: Everyone is completely happy. For those concerned about reaching this seventh heaven anywhere in the near future, no need to fret. Everywhere in the world, we are still considerably short of the upper bound. As you know, according to the World Happiness Report, where 10 is the top score, the highest countries average around 7.5 and the lowest 3.0.

And it's quite unlikely, of course, that we could ever get everyone to 10. Currently, in the three happiest countries—Finland, Denmark, and Norway—over a fourth of the population is at 9 or 10. A plausible goal might be to raise the global population to comparable levels.

So, striving for improvement isn't cancelled out by the happiness perspective.

"Maybe time for the happiness Olympics?!" asks Ted.

9.2 The Dashboard Approach

As support for GDP has waned, one alternative that has emerged is the so-called "dashboard" approach. This is easy to understand. Think of the dashboard of a car. It displays numerous indicators (perhaps more than most of us want), each reporting on a particular aspect of the car's functioning. Similarly, researchers assemble various economic, social, and other indicators of what they take to be well-being, and these constitute their dashboard. Of course, the dashboard in itself cannot tell us what's happened to overall well-being, just as there is no single measure of how well the car is functioning. From one year to the next, some well-being indicators will go up, others down, and in varying degrees. As a result, most well-being dashboards also include a summary index, where the items constituting the dashboard are averaged, albeit in an arbitrary way.

The United Nations' Human Development Index (HDI), introduced in 1990, was an important precursor of the dashboard approach, and it is still being published annually. The HDI is an average of just three items for each country: GDP per capita, life expectancy at birth, and mean years of schooling. The HDI, of course, gives a rather different picture of the world ranking of countries than GDP per capita alone, as was intended. The welfare states with their policy emphasis on the well-being of a country's people usually dominate the top ten ranking because of their attention to health and education, whereas the leaders in GDP per capita are typically the oil-rich Middle Eastern states. The United States ranks tenth on GDP per capita but falls to a tie with the United Kingdom for 15th on the HDI.

Since the launch of the HDI, a growing number of indexes have been proposed, usually with a much more extensive dashboard. As illustration, Table 9.1 lists some of these indexes and the number of component categories of well-being from which each index is constructed. Note that the number of component categories varies from as little as 3 to 54. Moreover, these component categories often differ considerably from one dashboard to the next, as is illustrated in Table 9.2. The Better Life Index, for example, includes things like political participation and work-life balance, while the Genuine Progress Indicator gives special attention to numerous environmental concerns.

Table 9.1   Some dashboard indexes of well-being (Handout #5)

Dashboard title	Number of principal component items
Better life index	11
Bhutan GNH index	9
Genuine progress index	26
Global peace index	23
Happy planet index	3
Human development index	3
Index of sustainable economic welfare	7
Legatum prosperity index	4
Multidimensional poverty index	10
Social progress index	54

Table 9.2   Principal categories of two dashboard measures (Handout #6)

Better life index [11 categories]	Genuine progress indicator [26 (selected categories)]
Housing conditions	*Economic*
Household income	Income inequality
Job security and unemployment	Consumption spending
Social support network	Stock of consumer durables
Education	Cost of underemployment
Quality of environment	
Involvement in democracy	*Environmental*
Health	Cost of water pollution
Life satisfaction	Cost of air pollution
Murder and assault rates	CO2 emissions
Work-life balance	Loss of wetlands
	Social
	Value of housework and parenting
	Cost of crime
	Value of volunteer work
	Cost of commuting

"To me, the dashboard idea seems kind of sketchy," reasons Keaton, "And you're not making it look any better, Professor Easterlin."

Well, one could argue that the dashboard proposals are actually a step in the right direction, because they lessen the importance of GDP. Moreover, the dashboard's specific indicators often offer insights into a variety of conditions that may affect people's well-being. But dashboards suffer from a number of problems, many the same as those afflicting GDP. First and foremost, as we have just seen, there is a wide range of competing conceptions of what goes into the dashboard. It's like the old days when scholars offered judgments about the content of "the Good Life" with as many judgments as judges.

Then, there is the problem of how to put the dashboard items together to construct a summary measure. Consider the Human Development Index, which as just mentioned has only three items. How does one average items that are, in fact, incommensurable? GDP, life expectancy, and schooling have different units of measurement: dollars for GDP, years of life for life expectancy, and years of education for schooling. If you think "years" makes life expectancy and schooling comparable, try this: If you average 60 years of life expectancy and 12 years of schooling, the answer is 36. So, what does *that* mean? You might as well average 60 pounds of steak and 12 pounds of nails. Attempts to evade this problem, say, by converting each measure to an index expressed in percentage terms, as is done with the HDI, only change the wording of the problem. In terms of people's well-being, is a 1% change in the index of steak output equivalent to a 1% change in the index of nail output?

Who decides on the dashboard's content and how to construct a summary measure? (Is it the dashboard of a 2020 Prius or a 1920 Model T?) Whatever the case, it's certain that the deciders aren't those whose well-being is being assessed. Given the variety of items on each dashboard, worries about subjectivism in analysis are hardly quashed. And whatever the eventual expanse of the dashboard, the resulting summary index is likely to be as unfathomable to the public as GDP and HDI.

"Maybe I should say goofy rather than sketchy," interjects Keaton.

Clearly, we need a primary measure of society's well-being. But dashboards, like GDP, are cooked up by outside observers who themselves are deciding what constitutes well-being; so, by extension, the policy relevance simply depends on the personal preconceptions of their creators. Happiness, in contrast, is what people themselves tell us is their well-being. If happiness were to become the principal gauge of societal well-being, public policy would shift toward programs more directly applicable to people's lives.

People's feelings would move center stage.

References and Further Reading

Easterlin, R. A. (2014). Why our happiness and satisfaction should supplant GDP in policy-making. Retrieved from http://theconversation.com/the-science-of-happiness-can-trump-gdp-as-a-guide-for-policy-57004

Kuznets, S., Epstein, L., & Jenks, E. (1941). *National income and its composition, 1919–1938* (Vol. 1). New York, NY: National Bureau of Economic Research.

Lemos, G. (2012). *The end of the Chinese dream: Why the Chinese people fear the future.* New Haven: Yale University Press.

Part III

Q & A

10

Who Is Happier: Young or Old? Women or Men?

10.1   What's Age Got to Do with It?

At this point, I invite the class to take over.

"*Fire away!*"

Jill supplies the curtain-raiser. "What happens to happiness as we get older?" Everyone waits.

"I know," bursts out Evan. "Happiness is U-shaped! Happiness goes down until age 50, and then goes up as you get older. I saw it on my iPad: 'If you're under 50, you haven't hit rock bottom.'"

Well, Evan, you're right that the media proclaims U-shaped happiness, but really, no single life cycle pattern of happiness prevails everywhere in the world. Yet there are some consistencies. In a number of developed countries, a wavelike rather than U-shape trajectory is common as people age. One of the waves does bottom out when people are still in their 50s—that's the trough of the supposed U-shape.

What sort of waves are we talking about? Ocean waves rolling to shore vary in height. This is also true of the life cycle waves in happiness, and sometimes there's a break in the succession of waves—something we see at the beach, too.

Here's the predominant pattern for lifetime happiness (Fig. 10.1). It starts with high happiness when most people are still in school (cheers from the class!). Enjoy it while you can, because happiness then diminishes, troughing when people are in their early to mid-20s (moans and groans). After that, happiness increases mildly to the mid- or late 30s, followed by a downturn that reaches the supposed rock bottom in the 50s. Finally, there is a rather sharp upturn that peaks in the 70s, succeeded by yet a third downturn. Most

R. A. Easterlin, *An Economist's Lessons on Happiness*,
https://doi.org/10.1007/978-3-030-61962-6_10

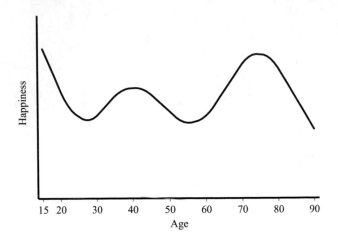

Fig. 10.1   Life cycle of happiness (Handout # 7)

of the variations are slight, but the initial decline and the final up and down movements are sizeable.

Peaks in happiness tend to occur in the teens, late 30s, and 70s while lows in the 20s, 50s, and beyond age 80.

You can see how this pattern reflects Cantril's findings that the most important things affecting personal happiness are one's economic situation, family, and health. The first trough is about jobs, occurring with the school-to-work transition. This is a difficult time for young people, marked by increased stress and anxiety as they leave school to search for work and take a first step up on the career ladder. (Scanning my students' suddenly glum faces, I can see how unwelcome this information is—they thought college was the hard part.)

Family circumstances mostly shape the course of happiness from the 20s through mid-life. As we've seen, happiness increases as people form partnerships and start families, usually in their mid-20s to late 30s (Chap. 5). The subsequent downturn reflects a gradual reversal in family well-being, a decline that parallels the rising incidence of divorce and the growth of single-parent families.

As people reach their 60s, retirement produces a considerable upward bump in happiness. But eventually, the so-called golden years of old age come to an end, as worsening health and the loneliness of increased widowhood take their toll, reducing happiness among the oldest-old. Nobel Laureate Angus Deaton puts it plainly: "[B]ad things begin to happen as you get older." So, whereas the much-touted U-shape implies endlessly increasing happiness in old age, the more likely wave pattern reflects physical realities and, frankly, confirms common sense.

Of course, individual experience can and does deviate from the average, sometimes substantially, and we've been talking only about the average pattern here. I've been fortunate enough to have a happy life, and the supposed rock bottom years of the 50s were my happiest, thanks to a second marriage.

"Well, then what's up with the U-shape?" Evan's not giving up. "How come it gets all this publicity?"

To start with, Evan, you're right to press on this, since it's so widely publicized. Can you guess? In happiness research, the U-shape is derived primarily from cross-section studies of happiness at ages running from around 20 to 65+. These cross-section studies are abundant, and almost all of them report the U-shaped finding, which explains the media attention it receives. As we know, cross-section studies aren't a reliable guide to what happens over time, and the U-shape is a prime example. We've seen how time-series studies often provide a very different—and more accurate—account, and this is true of lifetime happiness.

No surprise, then, that the wavelike pattern in Fig. 10.1 is based on time-series data reflecting the adult life span more fully than does cross-section study. For the most part, the pattern is from recently published research by two of my former graduate students, Robson Morgan and Kelsey J. O'Connor (Fig. 10.2). They analyzed data for 17 European countries with lengthy

Fig. 10.2 Economists at ease: Robson (*left*) and Kelsey (Courtesy of Robson Morgan and Kelsey J. O'Connor)

time-series spanning ages 20 to 80 and over—providing an additional 15 years of observations in older age. The wavelike pattern is an average of the 17 countries. A majority of the countries also show this pattern individually, but there are exceptions. And, let's remember, personal experience can deviate substantially from the average.

The Morgan-O'Connor results are supplemented here by Kelsey's findings from special tabulations of the European data as well as a study by economists Paul Frijters and Tony Beatton of three countries—Germany, Great Britain, and Australia—that follows the same individuals as they get older. These additional data make it possible to extend the life cycle range at both the younger end, adding ages 15–20, and at the older extreme, beyond age 65, and they are important in providing a fuller picture of the waves.

As you can see, one reason for the U-shape is the truncated time span in the cross-section studies—they are missing what happens before age 20 and after 65. But there are other features common to cross-section studies making for the U-shaped outcome. First, most researchers force the life-cycle happiness data to take the form of a quadratic equation, following mechanically in the footsteps of the initial cross-section study. (In an earlier life, I too was guilty of this procedure.) As a result, the life-cycle trajectory can have only a U- or hill shape. A wavelike pattern is not even possible. But if we jettison this rigid mathematical formula for a more flexible method—that of simply computing happiness for successive age groups from young to old—we find multiple ups and downs. The time-series studies drawn on here employ a method like this.

Second, most life-cycle studies treat a diverse array of variables unrealistically, because everything but age is taken as constant throughout the life course. In effect, this approach answers a seemingly somewhat fanciful question, to wit: If I compare younger, midlife, and older persons who are in exactly the same circumstances—economic situation, health, family life, and so on—how does their happiness differ? Now think of your own family, and you'll quickly realize that if you're interested in how happy people are over the life cycle, such a question is unrealistic. How many of you have parents and grandparents in the same life circumstances as you? If I may hazard a guess, the answer is "None."

The essence of life is that many circumstances change regularly with age. These changes aren't the same for every person, of course, but there are a lot of shared experiences at fairly similar ages—attending school, looking for a job, finding a partner, forming a family, retiring, experiencing health decline, and so on—and they impact people's happiness quite systematically. If you want to know the typical course of happiness as people age, you need to consider the effect of these regularly occurring changes throughout the life cycle. They're quantifiable and observable.

"But then, what's the point? Why bother with analyses that hold life circumstances constant?" Jane asks.

Despite the valid criticisms here, Jane, I do agree that there's a useful purpose for these analyses. The goal of such studies is to find out how changes in age, and only age, affect happiness—what some analysts call the "pure effect" of age. Researchers are asking, "What is the effect on happiness of the aging process itself?" To answer this, they compare, to the extent the data permit, people who are the same in every respect except age—they have the same gender, income, and education, the same everything, except age. How does happiness then differ when we compare the young, middle-aged, and old?

Let's look at heart disease rather than happiness, for purposes of illustration, because this shows how knowing the pure effect of age can be useful. We know that things like smoking and obesity are causes of heart disease. But we might also want a specific answer about age. For example, if we compare a 20-year-old with a 60-year-old who are the same with regard to known causes of heart disease, is the older person more prone to heart disease simply by virtue of his or her age? Is age itself a factor that makes for a greater risk of heart disease? The answer, of course, is yes. Knowing this leads to a helpful recommendation: Older persons should take greater precautions to reduce the chance of heart disease.

So, finding out how age by itself affects happiness is of interest, although we should recognize that age is really only a proxy for a more basic causal factor or factors connected to the aging process that we haven't yet identified, perhaps some biological condition. But, at the same time, knowing how age alone is related to happiness tells us nothing about the life-cycle experience of real persons. If we want to know *the typical trend in happiness* as people get older, it's essential to include the effects of changes in all of the life circumstances that change with age, as the time-series results here bring to the fore.

10.2   Who Are Happier? Women or Men?

This is Emily's question.

"You said jobs and family life matter for happiness. But you also suggested, I believe, that women care more about family life. So, is it different? Men's and women's happiness?"

Actually, in most developed countries, women and men are, in total, about equally happy. In fact, in the United States, the average happiness scores of women and men are basically identical. But then, Emily, there's the matter of the life cycle: This overall equality conceals important differences by age between women and men. Although both women and men basically follow the wavelike pattern, women are happier up to mid-life (half the class cheers); thereafter, men are happier (hurrahs from the other half).

The reversal in the relative happiness of women and men over the course of the life cycle is due at bottom to three things: compared with men, women generally marry at an earlier age, their life expectancy is greater, and their labor force participation is less. These three circumstances exist in almost every country throughout the world. It also seems, as Emily suggests, that the happiness of women does respond somewhat differently from that of men to the same family circumstances, such as having children. We saw some evidence of this in the results of Maggie Switek's research, where women's happiness was more affected by parenthood than men's (Chap. 5).

Age at marriage is important in accounting for the gender difference in life-cycle happiness, because marriage—or more accurately, finding a lifetime partner—raises happiness, as we know. Because women typically marry at a younger age than men, a larger proportion of women than men enjoy the upward boost of having a partner earlier in the life cycle, and, as a consequence, they are happier overall at that point in their lives. It's not until the two genders are in their 40s and 50s that the proportions married or cohabiting are roughly equal. In their 60s and thereafter, women are less likely to be married than men, so the positive partnership effect turns around in favor of men.

Women are less likely to be married than men at older ages, because, on average, women outlive men—in many developed countries, by five or more years. Hence, more and more women are left in a state of widowhood, and their happiness is reduced due to loss of a partner. Those men who are fortunate enough to be alive at older ages are, in contrast, more likely than women to still have a partner and are therefore happier than most women.

Likewise, older women benefit less from the retirement bump in happiness, because a smaller percentage has labor force experience compared with men. In the world as a whole, the labor force participation of women currently averages about two-thirds that of men; in the United States, about four-fifths. There are a few countries, mainly the Nordic and some in Eastern Europe, where women's labor force participation is almost the same as men's, and in those countries, there is little gender difference in the effect of the retirement bump. But in most countries, developed and less developed, a larger proportion of men are in the labor force, and thus men, on average, get a bigger boost in happiness from retiring.

"You talked earlier about the pure effect of age on happiness," Jane says, picking up on Emily's line of thought. "Is there a pure effect of gender? What if you compare women and men in the same circumstances? How does women's happiness compare to men's then?"

Good news for women on this, Jane. If we compare women and men in the same circumstances, women are as happy or happier than men (cheers again, some foot-stamping). A former graduate student of mine, Jackie Zweig (Fig. 10.3), looked into this question in 73 countries worldwide for which there were good data, comparing women and men in the same circumstances—age, income, occupation, education, health, marital status, and so

Fig. 10.3   Jackie with an armful (at soccer!) (Courtesy of Jacqueline Zweig)

on. In 62 of the 73 countries, women scored higher on happiness than men, significantly so in about a third of them. There was only one country, Costa Rica, in which men were demonstrably happier.

In the real world, of course, women, in general, have more adverse life circumstances than men. In nearly all countries, they suffer from lower incomes, less education, greater likelihood of widowhood, and worse reported health. All of these factors tend to reduce women's happiness relative to men. Jackie was quite aware of this at the outset of her study, and when her analysis additionally took these effects into account, women's happiness advantage shrank somewhat. But women still ended up as happy or happier than men in most countries. The number in which males were significantly happier rose only to 4 out of 73. So you see, Jane, your question reveals that the pure gender effect favoring women is quite strong—strong enough to very nearly offset the impact on happiness of a number of noticeably adverse life circumstances women often face compared with men.

10.3   Crossing the Finish Line

So, who is happier? Young or old, women or men? In either case, there's no simple answer. Early in the life cycle, women are happier; later on, men are. And both genders experience similar happiness ups and downs over the course of the life cycle, with no clear-cut advantage to young versus old.

References and Further Reading

Blanchflower, D. G., & Oswald, A. (2004). Well-being over time in Britain and the USA. *Journal of Public Economics, 88*(7–8), 1359–1386.

Easterlin, R. A. (2003). Happiness of women and men in later life: Nature, determinants, and prospects. In M. J. Sirgy, D. Rahtz, & A. C. Samli (Eds.), *Advances in quality-of-life theory and research* (pp. 13–26). Dordrecht, Netherlands: Kluwer Academic Publishers.

Frijters, P., & Beatton, T. (2012). The mystery of the U-shaped relationship between happiness and age. *Journal of Economic Behavior & Organization, 82*(2), 525–542.

Morgan, R., & O'Connor, K. J. (2017). Experienced life satisfaction in Europe. *Review of Behavioral Economics, 4*(4), 371–396.

Zweig, J. S. (2015). Are women happier than men? *Journal of Happiness Studies, 16*, 515–541.

11

More on Money and Happiness

11.1 Winning the Lottery

Owen is peering at me anxiously. I can see that the class isn't going to let me off the hook with a few questions about age and gender.

"When I was reading the Brickman article on health and happiness, it said that winning the lottery doesn't increase happiness. Is that correct?"

Well, that's what that article says, but let's remember, Owen, that the Brickman et al. analysis was done over four decades ago. To the credit of the authors, that study was, I believe, the first to look at the happiness effects of the lottery, so it was an important step in promoting happiness studies. Nevertheless, it was a cross-section analysis with very small sample sizes. Since then, time-series inquiries with much larger samples have been conducted. These studies consistently find that winning the lottery does increase happiness, but only if you hit it big. Small gains really don't matter, because they have no lasting effect on one's income situation. But large gains usually do.

It's easy to see why large lottery winnings increase happiness. All of a sudden, your income goes up a lot, and nobody else's changes. In this scenario, your income reference level stays the same because the incomes of others are constant, while your own income grows substantially. The result: Happiness increases. Needless to say, if everyone won the lottery, no one would be happier, because then the income reference level would increase as everyone's income rose. But we all know that it's not possible for everyone to win the lottery. The result? For the most part, the beneficiaries of big lottery payouts are happier than they were before.

Owen looks relieved.

© The Author(s), under exclusive license to Springer Nature Switzerland AG 2021
R. A. Easterlin, *An Economist's Lessons on Happiness*,
https://doi.org/10.1007/978-3-030-61962-6_11

11.2   Why Do Happiness and Income Fluctuate in Step?

"Early on, you said that happiness declines when there's an economic bust," Lily reminds us." That happiness and income go down together in the short run. Right?"

I nod, waiting to see where she is going.

"Yeah, but, if social comparison is the key thing keeping happiness from going up when income increases, why would happiness go down when people's incomes decrease? What about social comparison? If everyone's income decreases, then I'm no worse off than my neighbors, so wouldn't my happiness stay the same?"

Excellent work thinking through the analysis, Lily. The answer hinges on something we haven't discussed before: People react differently to a decrease compared with an increase in income.

You'll recall that the examples in my earlier lecture were always about the effect on happiness of an increase in income (Chap. 3). Recent statistical research by economist Jan-Emmanuel DeNeve and his colleagues demonstrates that the Paradox doesn't operate in both directions. When income goes up, happiness stays the same, but when income goes down, happiness decreases until income reaches rock bottom.

Diminishing happiness in the face of income loss is the result of what psychologists call "habituation." People become accustomed to a higher income, which gets built into their lifestyles, including their clothes, cars, homes, vacation destinations, and the debts they have incurred to finance their new ways of living. The lifestyle enabled by their newly increased income becomes, in effect, part of their selves, rapidly adapted to and incorporated into what they do and are. As a result, when folks experience a significant drop in income, as in a recession, they are unable to live their customary lives. They must adjust to a new, diminished lifestyle, and their happiness declines. The person who enjoyed vacationing in the Caymans and long nights in the tiki bar is not quite the same person he was before, because he can't do those things anymore. But as income bottoms out and recovery sets in, happiness is gradually restored, as income returns to its pre-recession level.

I distinguished previously between two types of comparison, inter- and intrapersonal (Chap. 4). As we've seen, when incomes increase, interpersonal (or social) comparison determines the income reference level: We are trying to keep up with the Joneses. But when incomes sink, intrapersonal comparison takes over. You can see how this is forced on a person when you think of fixed obligations like mortgage or car payments. When income declines, worries about meeting these fixed obligations become pressing; the fact that others are having the same problem doesn't make you feel any better. The problem of meeting fixed obligations forces people to turn inward. Thus, during an economic downturn, when incomes drop, happiness goes down too, because people's incomes are insufficient compared to what they're used to, their benchmark income. In a downturn, people's income reference levels are no longer what others are earning but what they themselves used to make, their personal best. The fact that one's peers are also feeling deprived doesn't make up for the loss in one's established way of living or help in meeting one's financial burdens. For the person who had gotten used to regularly attending home football games, there's no comfort in the fact that many others can no longer afford to either. He or she now feels deprived and less happy. It's just like the effect of a cohort's declining health as its members get older. All persons are less satisfied with their health, because they are all less healthy than they used to be. Similarly, in an economic contraction, everyone is less happy because they all have less money than they used to and share the same problems of debt repayment. ("All" is, of course, an exaggeration; I use it here for simplicity.)

Predictably, as recovery sets in and incomes rise back toward the pre-recession levels, so too does people's happiness, since they are now getting closer to their benchmark incomes. They're able once again to start going to football games and feel more secure about their finances, and their happiness gradually turns upward. So, happiness increases in the course of the business cycle recovery, until incomes surpass their previous benchmark levels. Does happiness continue a triumphant march up Everest? You know the answer. New highs in income, alas, don't increase happiness further, because social comparison muscles its way in, now replacing intrapersonal comparison in determining the income reference level. We are back to the dirty work of social comparison (Chap. 3). The person who upgrades to a Lexus is no happier than before, because all of his or her friends are doing the equivalent. Meantime, he or she is setting the stage for the next happiness decline via added debt liabilities.

Here, I'm giving you a simplified picture of what happens. In reality, of course, the switch between the two types of comparison is not instantaneous. Both when income is rising and when it is falling, there is a reasonably consistent, gradual transition from one type of comparison to the other.

"Wait!" says Lily. "In the case of health, you told us that intrapersonal comparison meant comparison with past experience. Now you are saying it's comparison with what's just been experienced. So, which is it?"

A good question, Lily—as usual, you're right on the ball. The fact is that the reference level for intrapersonal comparison can be in either the past or the present—it depends on what you're talking about. Let me try to clarify.

Let's think about intrapersonal comparison in terms of my earlier example, comparison with one's own personal best. In that case, we were talking about health, and in the case of health, one's best experience is usually in the past, sometimes the distant past. By contrast, in the case of income, one's highest income is generally quite recent.

There's a famous study of two medical procedures, colonoscopy and lithotripsy, by psychologist Daniel Kahneman and others that helps explain the difference between the benchmark levels of health and income. (Kahneman again: Remember him? An architect of the reference level concept [Chap. 3] and surveys of daily activities [Chap. 6]. No wonder he won the Nobel Prize!) In this case, Kahneman's inquiry demonstrates that a person's memory of the painfulness of a procedure depends primarily on how she or he felt at two points during the experience, at the peak and at the end, a concept known as the *peak-end rule*. Although this study was about medical procedures, I think the rule bears also on the benchmark levels of health and income.

Point in time is the crucial feature of Kahneman's study that is relevant here. Think about the life course of income and health in light of Kahneman's findings. The end of the experience occurs, of course, at the same point in time for both health and income, the present day. But the peak is quite different. For health, the peak or personal high is in the past, while for income it is typically in the present. To illustrate from my own experience: When I was in my 20s, I could pass a football and play tennis reasonably well. Those days are gone forever; now I am lucky to be able to limp around the golf course. In contrast, my income has risen rather steadily over my career. Physical decline is a universal fact of aging, whereas incomes are likely to rise with career experience and advancement. Hence, the benchmark for health differs from that for income, because its early peak pulls the benchmark back into the past. In contrast, for income, up until retirement, the peak generally coincides with the most recent (end) situation. The reference level for health, then, is in the past, while that for income, where the peak and end times are usually the same, is the present.

11.3   Greener Grass? Misremembering Past Happiness

Emma has an incisive question.

"Why don't people learn from experience and realize that more income won't make them happier? You'd think they'd eventually realize that it's an illusion to think that money and happiness go together."

Good reasoning, Emma. The answer to your question hinges on the income reference level that a person uses to evaluate her or his past experience. We all know now that an upward economic movement raises our income benchmark. During times of economic growth, most incomes trend upward. Social comparison, therefore, will be based on progressively new and higher benchmark levels of income. This higher benchmark income then becomes the basis for evaluating earlier years as well as the present. This is the key to answering your question. When people are asked, "How happy were you 5 years ago?", they assess the past situation based on the current, higher benchmark, not in light of the reference level that actually prevailed 5 years before. They are now enjoying a more plentiful living than 5 years previously, and they assess that prior situation in the light of their current greater abundance.

Does the past usually look worse than the present in this scenario, when economic growth has been pushing up the income benchmark? You bet! As a result, people typically say they were less happy 5 years ago than they are now. In US surveys conducted annually over a 25-year period in the late twentieth century, people almost invariably reported that they were less happy 5 years before. But in truth, 5 years before, their feelings were based on the lower-income reference level that prevailed at that time, not the new, higher level, and they were actually just as happy then as now.

We looked at the trend in American happiness since the end of World War II early on (Chap. 3), and it has been flat or even slightly negative, confirming that happiness in the past has actually been as great or greater than present happiness, contrary to people regularly reporting they were less happy 5 years ago. Since people incorrectly evaluate the past, thinking that they were less happy when, in fact, they were just as happy as in the present, they don't learn that higher income does not increase happiness. In a nutshell, people do not learn from experience that more money won't make them happier because they underestimate their past happiness. In the happiness realm, Emma, this is why people don't learn from experience.

This tendency to evaluate the past in terms of present circumstances isn't unique to happiness. It also occurs in the political arena. For example, political attitudes were surveyed at the beginning of a decade and then again 10 years later for the same set of persons. In the end-of-decade survey, respondents were also asked what their attitudes had been 10 years earlier. It turned out that those whose attitudes had actually changed reported their past attitudes to be the same as the present ones, even though they were, in fact, different. They recalled their past political attitudes based on their current point of view, just as people assess their past happiness in terms of their present circumstances.

11.4   Greener and Greener? Mispredicting Future Happiness

The present income reference level is the benchmark not only for assessments of past happiness but also for predictions about future happiness. When asked, "How happy do you expect to be 5 years from now?", most people reply that they expect to be happier. They are optimistic because they are comparing their presumed income situation 5 years hence, which, for most people, is higher than currently, with their present income reference level. They don't understand that, as other people's incomes rise along with their own, that reference level will also increase and offset the positive effect on happiness of their own growth in income. Implicitly, they make the same faulty assumption as when they are asked whether more income will make them happier: namely, that their income will increase but that the incomes of others will not. Thus, they predict an increase in happiness. Yet as we know, most incomes rise together over time, boosting the income reference level. Because the income reference level—fundamentally, the incomes of others—is growing along with individual income, happiness remains unchanged.

11.5   Is All Utility Created Equal?

Perhaps this rings a bell—that our expectations don't always line up with outcomes. It's a familiar finding in social psychology, where the discrepancy has been the subject of considerable study. Researchers distinguish formally between *decision utility*, the expected satisfaction resulting from a particular choice, and *experienced utility*, the satisfaction actually realized. We all know from personal experience that decision and experienced utility are not necessarily the same. We go for the lemon tart on the dessert menu and find it

soggy and overly sweet, stealing envious glances at the Napoleon being gob-
bled up by our daughter. The experienced utility of the not-tart tart did not
come within the horizon of the decision utility!

The two utility concepts succinctly express our misconception of the effect
on happiness of an increase in income. The decision utility (or expected outcome) of more personal income is greater happiness; however, the experienced
utility (or actual result) is unchanged happiness, because others' incomes also
increase. Social comparison leads to experienced utility ending up less than
decision utility. The negative effect on happiness of the increase in others'
incomes offsets the positive effect of the growth in one's own income.

Mainstream economic theory overlooks the distinction between the two
concepts, equating experienced with decision utility. The *theory of revealed
preference*, a linchpin of mainstream theory, posits that people are trying to
maximize their utility—in this case, their happiness—and that if people
choose situation Y in preference to situation X when both situations are within
reach, that's because Y has greater utility than situation X. In other words,
they choose the situation that they think will lead to greater happiness. The
theorist would argue that, having made that choice, they must be happier,
that is, experienced utility is the same as decision utility. Of course, we don't
know the true utility of anything we've chosen until we experience it, though
the factors that make or break the equation vary. For the lemon tart, too much
sugar and too little oven temperature, maybe? In the case of happiness, once
social comparison is added to the analysis, as it should be, the assumed iden-
tity between decision and experienced utility falls apart. Because of social
comparison, people fail to predict correctly the outcome of their decisions,
and experienced utility falls short of decision utility.

11.6   Concluding Thoughts

The distinction between decision and experienced utility harks back to the
debate about the ultimate purpose of economic analysis with which I began.
Remember that the Italian economist Vilfredo Pareto asserted that economics
is a science of choice, not well-being—in effect, that economics stops with
decision utility. Pareto's view encapsulates the disciplinary perspective
throughout much of the twentieth century. But these days, more and more
economists, not just those researching happiness, are interested in outcomes.
In other words, they are interested in experienced utility. Thus, Ben Bernanke,
former chair of the US Federal Reserve Board, says, "The ultimate purpose of
economics is … to understand and promote the enhancement of well-being."

For those who subscribe to Pareto's view, happiness has no place in economics. For those agreeing with Bernanke, happiness is what economics is all about—and you can bet that happiness economists are in Bernanke's camp.

References and Further Reading

De Neve, J. E., Ward, G., De Keulenaer, F., van Landeghem, B., Kavetsos, G., & Norton, M. I. (2018). The asymmetric experience of positive and negative economic growth: Global evidence using subjective well-being data. *Review of Economics and Statistics, 100*(2), 362–375.

Lindqvist, E., Ostling, R., & Cesarini, D. (2020). Long-run effects of lottery wealth on psychological well-being. *Review of Economic Studies*, 87(6), 2703–2726.

Lipset, S. M., & Schneider, W. (1987). *The confidence gap: Business, labor, and government in the public mind* (Revised ed., pp. 130–131). Baltimore MD: Johns Hopkins University Press.

Redelmeier, D. A., & Kahneman, D. (1996). Patients' memories of painful medical treatments: Real- time and retrospective evaluations of two minimally invasive procedures. *Pain, 66*(1), 3–8.

12

What About Democracy, Religion, Charity, Volunteering, Etc.?

12.1 What's Most Important?

The class seems restive. As I step to the podium, some whispering and raising of hands. But they're not about to wait for me today.

"From what I've read," Tyler blurts out, "there's a whole bunch of things that you haven't even mentioned that make people happy. Like democracy, culture, less income inequality, a healthier environment. What about those things?"

"Yeah," Peter chimes in. "And also, you've talked about immediate family, but not relatives, friends, neighbors—stuff like that."

"I think helping others through giving or volunteering is important. And what about religion?" adds Gretchen.

OK—points well taken!

I'll talk about some of those things shortly, but first let me restate where I'm coming from. Remember that, in the beginning of this class, we discussed Hadley Cantril's survey of the concerns most important for happiness (Chap. 2). Cantril first asked people about their hopes: Imagine the future in the best possible light, that of perfect happiness. The survey also asked a similar question about their fears: Envision the future in the worst possible light. And recall that the survey was completely open-ended, since nothing guided the answers toward preordained possibilities. So, thinking about what did or didn't make them happy, people just volunteered what came to mind at the time.

To me, these answers tell us what's foremost in determining people's happiness and, as a consequence, what analysts, policy-makers, and everyday individuals should especially focus on to improve happiness.

R. A. Easterlin, *An Economist's Lessons on Happiness*,
https://doi.org/10.1007/978-3-030-61962-6_12

Why haven't we discussed many of the things that Tyler, Peter, and Gretchen bring up? Because people seldom or never cite them in Cantril's survey responses.

At the outset, we saw that in every 1 of the 13 countries Cantril surveyed, 3 broad concerns topped the list: the respondents' economic situation, family, and health. Fortunately, Cantril gives considerably more detail about the types of things included under each of these headings as well as any things that respondents mention that do not fall in these categories. Let me spell these out, so that you can get a better sense of what people say about their happiness. Below, in parentheses next to each of Cantril's items, I've indicated the number of countries out of the total of 13 for which at least 10% of a country's respondents cite the item.

The principal items that Cantril identifies under *personal economic situation*:

A decent or improved standard of living (13)   Have own farm or business (10)

Have own house (12)   Have modern conveniences/ wealth (8)

Steady or congenial employment (10)   More leisure (5)

The list is somewhat shorter for family:

Children (13)   Happy old age (4)

Happy family life (12)   Relatives (2)

And shorter still for health:

Good health—self (11)   Good health—family (7)

Our three broad categories of leading concerns thus break down into 12 more detailed concerns.

Besides these 12 detailed concerns, only a few others are mentioned in Cantril's survey by 10% or more of a country's population, and the number of countries in which these other matters reach that percentage is small. Here are these other items and the number of countries that meet the 10% cutoff:

Peace (4)   Achieve sense of personal worth (1)

Self-development or improvement (3)   Acceptance by others (1)

Emotional stability and maturity (1)   Resolution of religious problems (1)

Be a normal, decent person (1)

Once in a while, respondents mention things like freedom and social justice, but in no country are these cited by at least 10% of respondents.

What is striking about the Cantril's findings is the down-to-earth nature of people's frequently identified concerns. Mostly, it's the things that take up their daily lives that are central to their happiness and that they think they have some ability to control. In very poor countries, it may come down to worries about putting bread on the table while in richer, seeing the doctor when the need arises. But in all countries, it's things that are foremost in their lives that matter most for happiness. Note also the close-to-home character of the responses. Immediate family is mentioned often; relatives make the 10% bar in only two countries, and friends and neighbors, not at all.

So that's why I've been focusing throughout on mundane matters of money, family, and health—because, over and over again, people tell us that these everyday things are most important for their happiness.

But let's go back to some of the things that Tyler, Peter, and Gretchen brought up at the beginning of class: friends, neighbors, income inequality, democracy, culture, the environment, volunteerism, and religion. For most of these, some research supports the view that they contribute to people's happiness, but that research is virtually always cross-sectional, and as we know cross-section associations are not necessarily a reliable guide to what happens over time.

Let's start with a couple of examples. (A word of warning: At this point, I part company with a number of colleagues in the economics of happiness, who are more accepting of purely cross-sectional findings.)

12.2 Self-Evident Truths: The Matter of Democracy

Democracy is defined as a system of government in which power is vested in the people and exercised by them through freely elected representatives. It contrasts with other forms of government, most notably autocracy, where power is exercised by one person or group of persons. The question here comes down to whether being able to vote for a representative in political decision-making increases happiness.

There are very few studies of the effect of democracy on happiness. The most-cited one is by two economists, Bruno Frey and Alois Stutzer, who investigated differences in happiness among 26 Swiss cantons (geographic districts into which Switzerland is divided). After eliminating many other possible sources of happiness differences among the cantons, they found happiness to be significantly higher in more democratic cantons.

In their analysis the measure of democracy is the possibility of getting an initiative or referendum on the ballot; this differs among cantons in things like the number of signatures required and the length of the period in which the signatures must be collected. Cantons that had fewer barriers to initiating a referendum—fewer signatures required and a longer period to collect them—were considered to be more democratic and turned out to be happier. The article does not tell us how many residents of cantons with greater or fewer barriers actually took advantage of the opportunity to initiate a referendum, something that might give us an inkling of the significance to people of this privilege.

In terms of my personal experience in the United States, I find it somewhat hard to accept that happiness is greater if you live in a place where it's easier to get a referendum on the ballot. When I moved to California, I had no idea that it is much simpler to introduce a referendum here than in most states. I found this out at election time, because the sample ballot that was distributed in advance contained more than ten initiatives on a variety of issues on which I was ill-informed and needed a fair amount of time to get up to speed. I cannot say that discovering that the possibility was now easier than before of my placing a referendum on the ballot did much for my happiness, and I rather doubt that most Californians feel much differently. Launching a referendum seems like something that generates little interest or thought among most people most of the time. (By contrast, knowing enough about these initiatives in advance of election day is a potential source of anxiety, though probably with no measurable effect on happiness.)

A much better test of whether democracy affects happiness is one I discussed earlier, the time-series study of the establishment of democracy in South Africa (Chap. 7). The country held its first democratic election in April 1994. One month later, a survey was conducted that included questions on both happiness and life satisfaction. By both measures, happiness of the black population soared at that time. But, as noted sociologist Valerie Moller, who was responsible for the survey, observes: "[P]ost-election euphoria was short-lived. Satisfaction levels have since returned to ones reminiscent of those under the former regime." Although the establishment of democracy in South Africa led to a temporary spike in happiness, there was no enduring effect.

We would all like to believe that democracy increases happiness. However, while acknowledging our ideals, let's continue putting the evidence first. In the case of South Africa, the data simply don't show a correlation between democracy and happiness. This result is consistent with Hadley Cantril's findings that people rarely mention political conditions as a source of happiness. When it comes to what determines happiness, immediate personal concerns apparently override types of governance.

Not surprisingly, the class is less than enthusiastic.

"Wait a minute," says Tim. "It's bad enough when you tell us that socialism makes people happier. But now you're just contradicting yourself! Now you're saying democracy doesn't count. So how can socialism?"

That's not quite what I said, Tim, but you bring up something important. Before, we looked specifically at whether *government policies*, not any particular political system, could increase people's happiness (Chaps. 7 and 8). What we saw was that, based on the evidence, specific policies—in particular, employment and safety net policies—lead to higher levels of happiness. However, we also saw that *different kinds of political regimes can institute these policies*. So, welfare state policies with a positive effect on happiness have been established in the Nordic democracies, in Eastern European socialist states, and even in authoritarian Middle East Gulf states. The common cause of happiness in every case is not the type of regime, whether democratic, socialist, or authoritarian, but the policies directed toward people's foremost economic, health, and family concerns.

The evidence, in short, reveals that specific policies make for happier nations, not type of governance, democracy (regretfully) included.

12.3 Do Cultural Differences Undermine Happiness Comparisons?

Cantril's survey results also underscored that, irrespective of cultural differences, people's concerns with respect to happiness are largely the same throughout the world. This by no means implies that tastes are identical everywhere. No doubt, when people decide what to put on the table at mealtime, the favorite dishes in China and Iceland aren't similar. But in both countries, actually putting food on the table is critical for happiness.

Let's now go back to the time-series evidence from the transition experiences of China and Eastern Europe, areas with starkly different cultures, because this comparison further illuminates the likeness across cultures in the determinants of happiness.

At the start of the transition in both China and Eastern Europe, economic restructuring and its consequent effects, including appalling upsurges in unemployment and dissolution of the social safety net, produced the same result: Citizens of these countries expressed new day-to-day worries, and surveys registered a marked decline in life satisfaction. Subsequently, gradual economic recovery and patches to the social safety net led to an upturn in life satisfaction. Despite differences in language, tastes, and beliefs between China and Eastern Europe, similar economic and policy circumstances produced U-shaped patterns of life satisfaction in both places. The parallel happiness findings in China and Eastern Europe during the transition underscore the two regions' agreement about what principally leads to life satisfaction. No one can rule out possible cultural influences on happiness; nonetheless, people everywhere place everyday matters at the top of their lists of sources of life satisfaction, and these close-to-home concerns largely override cultural effects on happiness.

12.4   Fair and Square: Environment, Income Inequality, Social Capital

China's transition experience also implicitly responds to some of the other questions of the class.

To start with, there is the environment. All of us have seen pictures of Chinese cityscapes draped in densely polluted air. The prodigious growth of coal production and consumption is the principal villain here, steadily driving up air pollution over the past three decades.

Income inequality, too, trends steadily upward in China from 1990 onward. It's certainly logical to expect, as many of the students do, that happiness would slide consistently downward, given these strong, simultaneous upward trends in environmental pollution and income inequality. Yet as we know, the happiness pattern is actually U-shaped. In fact, since the turn of the twenty-first century, life satisfaction in China has trended upward, while air pollution and inequality continued to worsen. Clearly, China's time-series evidence does not support the view that the environment and income distribution are major determinants of happiness.

The term "social capital" has become widely known as a result of Harvard sociologist Robert D. Putnam's 2000 book Bowling Alone. It refers to the benefits fostered by extensive social networks—that is, by wide-ranging relationships with friends, neighbors, fellow members of churches, clubs, civic associations, and the like. Stronger and more numerous relationships (the opposite of "bowling alone") are believed to foster benefits like greater trust in others, heightened civic cooperation (not cheating on benefit claims or taxes), and disapproval of actions like attempted bribery of public officials. In a joint article with Canadian economist John Helliwell, Putnam found a significant positive cross-section association in both Canada and the United States between life satisfaction, on one hand, and, on the other, trust, memberships, and several additional measures of social capital.

Join up and be happy!

Would it were so. Once again, China's experience since 1990 makes it possible to see whether the social capital-life satisfaction association holds up over time. We have data for trust in others, civic cooperation, and disapproval of bribery for the period since 1990. None correlate with the U-shaped course of happiness. Trust in others, for example, is going up at the time when happiness plunges to its lowest point—a negative relationship. Civic cooperation changes very little from 1990 to 2002 and then worsens as life satisfaction improves—again, a negative association. As with the environment and income inequality, social capital fails a time-series test as a principal determinant of self-reported happiness. In contrast, measures of employment conditions and the safety net in China fit the down and up movement of life satisfaction.

12.5   Inspiration and Afterglow: Religion, Volunteerism, Giving

In the flurry of questions at the start of class, Gretchen's were about belief and altruism—important topics for us all, so let's move on to them.

Numerous cross-section studies identify a positive relationship between religiosity, as measured by frequency of engagement in religious activities, and happiness. The relationship is much the same irrespective of the nature of one's faith, whether Christian, Muslim, Buddhist, Jewish, and so on. A much more limited number of inquiries report that happiness is greater among those exhibiting altruistic behaviors, such as volunteering for charity work and donating money. A study of East Germany, for example, found that more regular volunteer work was associated with greater happiness. An American analysis reported that happiness was higher among those who spent more on gifts for others and charitable donations.

If such studies are correct in suggesting that religious belief and altruistic behavior can increase people's happiness, it's by no means clear from a policy viewpoint how to act on such findings. Should we exhort people to be religious, to help and care for others? Such activities are likely to take time and money—for those not already involved, it's uncertain that the sacrifices required would increase, rather than decrease, happiness. Indeed, there is evidence that happiness is less among those who spend more time caring for close kin.

Furthermore, there's some evidence that the satisfaction resulting from altruism is not a product of specific behaviors but a reflection of personality traits. A study on volunteerism by psychologist Hannah R. King and associates provides evidence specifically to this effect. She first establishes a positive association between volunteering and both physical and mental health, a result that is consistent with happiness research demonstrating a positive impact of volunteering. (We can take mental health here as a rough proxy for happiness.) However, she then adds to the explanatory analysis the Big Five personality characteristics that we talked about earlier (Chap. 5). The result is that volunteering no longer has a significant relation to mental health, while the expected Big Five personality traits do. Extroversion is positively related and neuroticism negatively related to mental health, replicating the relations to happiness cited earlier. In King's words, "These results indicate that volunteering may be related to health outcomes because of the personality characteristics of volunteers, not the volunteering experience in and of itself."

In my teaching and in this book, I downplay the positive relation to happiness of religion, volunteering, and giving, because personality appears to be so much in play, and personality is not easily changed. Most certainly, personality will always factor into a person's happiness. Nonetheless, studies like those of China and Eastern Europe highlight the extent to which, irrespective of the personalities of individual citizens, social policies that address everyday concerns raise happiness overall.

12.6   Exceptional Events

One thing the class has overlooked is the possible impact of exceptional events on happiness. These fall into two different categories, reflecting their highly disparate consequences for people's lives: short-lived mega-events like sports championships and rock concerts and major catastrophes like hurricanes, earthquakes, and acts of terror. Studies of the effect on happiness of these disparate sorts of event are rare but informative. Let's take a look here at some representative findings.

On the basis of existing evidence, mega-events typically have short-term effects that are chiefly captured in experiential measures, those reflecting hourly or daily moods. When Spain won the 2000 World Cup, the team's fans experienced an emotional high. But this elation lasted only about 4 days. Earlier in the tournament, Germany eliminated England, thereby generally depressing England's fans. The disappointment, however, lasted less than 4 days.

Catastrophic events are an entirely different kettle of fish, leaving a noticeable mark on the evaluative measures, those reflecting people's overall satisfaction with their lives. Most studies find a sizeable decrease in happiness at the time of the disaster and for some period thereafter, followed by an eventual return to pre-disaster levels. An example is the impact on happiness of Hurricane Katrina, which assaulted the US Gulf Coast on August 29, 2005. Over 1.1 million people were evacuated, a displacement of population comparable to the Dust Bowl migrations of the 1930s. Although the storm directly hit the Mississippi Gulf Coast, New Orleans especially sustained great damage, with massive flooding in many areas as a result of levee breaches. More than 60% of the city's housing stock was destroyed.

Fortunately, there is a longitudinal survey for New Orleans following the same persons from 1 year before the hurricane to 1 and 4 years after. The basic finding is that, compared to its pre-hurricane value, happiness is markedly less 1 year after the hurricane but 4 years later has recovered to its initial level. Although the sample, which consists of young low-income mothers, is not representative of the population as a whole, the happiness trajectory is like those observed for other natural catastrophes. The pattern, of course, is the average for all those surveyed. Not surprisingly, those who experienced the death of a family member or who lost their homes sustained a more lasting negative impact. There are no comparable longitudinal happiness studies for the many evacuees who ended up living elsewhere, but a study of 101 adults who evacuated to Louisville, Kentucky, found that 1 year after the hurricane, a majority were suffering from depression and anxiety, much like their New Orleans counterparts.

12.7   The Thumbnail Happiness Test

The social sciences abound with studies of the things making for happiness. But to assess the value of any argument, ask yourself the following:

- What evidence is cited for any given factor? Is it cross-sectional? Usually it is, which raises the question of whether it holds up over time. (See "democracy".)

- Is the factor perhaps a proxy for something more basic like personality? If so, what policy conclusions, if any, can we draw? (See "volunteering".)
- Is the measure of happiness evaluative (happiness with life in general) or experiential (happiness in the past week)? (See "exceptional events.") If experiential, is there anything by way of policy that can or should be done? (Doubtful.)

None of this is to say that factors such as those discussed in this class meeting do not matter at all. Remember that we're looking at concerns mentioned by at least 10% of the population. Certainly, there are individuals for whom things like volunteering or reducing air pollution may be important for their happiness. My point is that not all sources of happiness are created equal. I've focused here on those that matter most to most people. First things first!

References and Further Reading

Clark, A., & Llekes, O. (2005). *Deliver us from evil: Religion as insurance.* Paris, France: Paris School of Economics.

Dunn, E., Aknin, L., & Norton, M. I. (2008). Spending money on others promotes happiness. *Science, 319*(5870), 1687–1688.

Frey, B. S., & Stutzer, A. (2000). Happiness, economy, and institutions. *Economic Journal, 110*, 918–938.

Helliwell, J. F., & Putnam, R. D. (2004). The social context of well-being. *Philosophical Transactions: Biological Science, 359*, 1435–1446.

King, H. R., Jackson, J. J., Morrow-Howell, N., & Oltmanns, T. F. (2015). Personality accounts for the connection between volunteering and health. *The Journals of Gerontology: Series B, 70*(5), 691–697.

Meier, S., & Stutzer, A. (2006). *Is volunteering rewarding in itself?* Boston, MA: Federal Reserve Bank of Boston, Center for Behavioral Economics and Decision-Making.

Moller, V. (2007). Researching quality of life in a developing country: Lessons from the South Africa case. In I. Gough & J. A. McGregor (Eds.), *Wellbeing in developing countries: From theory to research* (pp. 242–258). Cambridge, UK: Cambridge University Press.

Putnam, R. D. (2000). *Bowling alone: The collapse and revival of American community.* New York, NY: Simon and Schuster.

Van den Berg, B., & Ferrer-i-Carbonell, A. (2007). Monetary valuation of informal care: The well-being valuation method. *Health Economics, 16*(11), 1227–1244.

13

Who to Believe? Psychology or Economics?

13.1 Explaining Happiness

Ada is the rare psychology major who has ventured into economics.

"I think," she says, "that you're not being fair to psychology. You make it sound like economics is always right."

"I'm sorry, Ada. That's not at all how I feel. The two disciplines do often differ, but neither is always right. Economics sometimes has the best of it, at other times, psychology; and every so often neither is right, but a combination of the two may make sense. Let me try to clarify by discussing some of the differences between the two fields of study. Suppose we start with their views on the causes of happiness."

In truth, neither discipline is completely right on causes. However, we can build on the predominant theories in economics and psychology to obtain a better understanding. Of course, scholars' theoretical commitments aren't unanimous in either discipline, but nevertheless, disciplines exhibit central tendencies. The prevailing view in psychology is dubbed "setpoint theory," whereas that in economics might be called "more is better." The two theories lead to divergent views about whether life circumstances have lasting effects on happiness. The psychologists typically say "no," the economists, "yes."

In general, psychologists hold that each individual has a stable level of happiness. This is called the "setpoint," and it reflects personality, given essentially at birth by one's genes. As the prominent psychologist Richard E. Lucas professes, "The assumption that happiness setpoints exist has guided much of the current theory and research [in psychology]" (Lucas et al. 2004, 8). On this view, life events like unemployment or new employment, serious injury or

R. A. Easterlin, *An Economist's Lessons on Happiness*,
https://doi.org/10.1007/978-3-030-61962-6_13

disease, improved health, and loss or gain of a partner temporarily deflect persons above or below their setpoint, but in a short time, people habituate to their new conditions, and they revert to their original happiness setpoint. We can put this neatly in terms of our theoretical discussion so far: Psychology claims that reference levels, on the basis of which persons evaluate their individual situation, adjust rapidly and completely to life events. So if, say, your happiness drops due to a child's death, you quickly get used to the situation, your benchmark for evaluating your family circumstances adjusts correspondingly, and happiness returns to its original level.

Earlier, I showed how this view has been applied to health and marriage (Chaps. 4 and 5). Remember that, in one study, psychological researchers held that those who have become quadriplegics due to an accident adjust rapidly to their new circumstances, ending up as happy as they were before the accident. And in another study, the findings suggested that marriage produces an upward bump in happiness, but then the partners quickly habituate to their new situation and revert to their pre-marriage happiness levels. Indeed, some setpoint advocates go so far as to claim that life circumstances have a negligible role to play in a theory of happiness. In effect, they assert that genes and personality are the whole story, together establishing a person's basic level of happiness throughout life.

Philosophically, unmodified setpoint theory faces the same ethical dilemma as Calvinist predestination, according to which some people are damned at birth, without a chance for salvation. In other words, strong setpoint theory evinces a determinist perspective, because no actions or adjustments can make a difference to individuals. Thus, in happiness studies, unmodified setpoint theory leads to nihilism, since there's no hope of improving subjective well-being via either public policy or personal decisions. It implies that any government measures aimed at improving people's life circumstances, such as strengthening health care or expanding employment opportunities, will have only a transient effect on well-being: In short order, each individual will return to the setpoint established at birth by her or his genes. By the same token, if setpoint theory is correct, there is little an individual can do to improve his or her happiness, because it is formed at the start of life.

Economists, by contrast, are strong believers in the importance of life circumstances, holding particularly that income is a primary determinant of well-being. Their focus on income is reflected in allegiance to GDP. As we have seen, the prevailing view in economics is revealed preference theory, which might simply be called "more is better"—the more you have, the happier you are (Chap. 11).

This theory implies that increasing income improves well-being and that public policy measures aimed at increasing the income of society as a whole—that is, economic growth—lead to greater well-being. Economists do recognize that well-being depends on a variety of circumstances besides one's material conditions, but typically, they assume that, if income increases substantially, overall well-being, or social welfare, will move in the same direction. The original authority for this was British welfare economist A. C. Pigou, who declared almost a century ago that "there is a clear perception that changes in economic welfare [that is, GDP per capita] indicate changes in social welfare in the same direction, if not in the same degree" (Pigou 1932, 3).

Undoubtedly, if the evidence points wholesale to either or both of these approaches, then we're bound to accept it. So then: What is the evidence for the merits of either or both of the two theories? We've seen the answers (Chaps. 3–5). Income has a nil relation to happiness (psychology wins); health and family life are positively related to happiness (economics wins).

Neither discipline carries the day!

The theory presented earlier, which draws on the views of both disciplines, reconciles these differing results. Start with the simple economic model, according to which an increase in a person's income increases happiness. Add from psychology what we've learned about how people evaluate a situation, namely, via an internal benchmark or reference level. Reference levels, in turn, depend on both interpersonal and intrapersonal comparisons. In the case of income, *inter*personal comparison dominates the reference level for assessing one's situation. As the economy trends upward, the positive impact on happiness of an increase in one's own income is undercut by a corresponding increase in the income reference level, because the incomes of others also rise. The outcome: Happiness is unchanged. In the case of health and family life, *intra*personal comparison serves primarily as the reference level, and it is fairly fixed. As a result, improvements in health and family life produce increases in happiness. Unlike income, gains in these life circumstances are not offset by corresponding changes in reference levels.

Thus, adding psychology's concept of benchmark or reference levels to the simple economic model yields a theory that explains the seemingly inconsistent results for income vis-à-vis health and family circumstances.

Neither discipline in itself tells the full story, but the two together do.

13.2   What People Say…

Can we trust what people say? In economics, subjective testimony—people's opinions, beliefs, attitudes, and feelings—has long been suspect. How can these things constitute viable evidence in the discipline's research? Needless to say, many economists look askance at data on self-reported happiness.

For psychologists, however, subjective testimony is no problem; indeed, many make their living precisely by listening to what people say. But as we shall see, economists have traditionally dismissed personal views of the sort obtained in survey research, insisting that only actual behavior is meaningful as evidence (Chap. 15). There has been some modification of this position in the last few decades, during which public opinion surveys have gradually come into use in economic research. Nonetheless, economists still often treat survey statistics as second-class evidence—"soft" as opposed to "hard" objective data, such as that on income and education. Nobel Laureate Richard Thaler, one of the founders of behavioral economics, explicitly criticizes this attitude. Writing in 2015, he asserts that, even "to this day, the phrase 'survey evidence' is rarely heard in economic circles without the necessary adjective 'mere,' which rhymes with 'sneer'" (Thaler 2015, 47). To borrow from another Nobel Laureate, George Akerlof, "The hardness police rule out soft data as inadmissible evidence" (Akerlof 2020, 415).

It seems hard to believe that economics would shut the door on subjective testimony, since how people feel about things actually determines their behavior, and feelings can only be accessed via self-reports. Human beings are, after all, highly evolved, and their behavior cannot be easily separated from their thoughts and feelings. A person's income may be large or small in absolute amount, but *it is how the individual perceives it*—that is, whether or not the amount is satisfactory—that is critical to understanding his or her emotions and behavior. In rejecting or devaluing subjective testimony, economics has been discounting evidence providing valuable insights into people's actions. Clearly, when it comes to open-minded recognition of the legitimacy of subjective testimony, psychology has the best of it.

13.3   Vetting Happiness, Gauging Happiness

Psychology has also led the way in the assessment of happiness measures. Tests developed by psychologists on reliability (consistency over short periods) and validity (truthfulness) of self-reported happiness have helped to establish that happiness measures are meaningful. Since we laid this groundwork at the outset (Chap. 2), I won't repeat it here. It is, however, a major contribution by psychology that has encouraged the general acceptance of happiness measures, even in economics.

You'll also recall that there are two categories of happiness measure, evaluative and experiential. Evaluative measures, those we have relied on here, are overall assessments of one's state of life, whereas experiential measures are of one's momentary mood at or shortly before the time of the survey.

Both disciplines use both types of measure, but, as between the two, economists lean strongly toward the evaluative, while psychologists tend to favor the experiential. Two major reports relating to happiness illustrate this fundamental difference. One is the 2009 *Report by the Commission on the Measurement of Economic Performance and Social Progress* (sometimes called the "Stiglitz-Sen-Fitoussi Report") prepared largely by economists; the other is a 2013 report, *Subjective Well-Being: Measuring Happiness, Suffering, and other Dimensions of Experience,* written mainly by psychologists and published by the US National Research Council. The two reports also reflect a general divergence in approaches to happiness studies on opposite sides of the Atlantic. Evaluative gauges typify European research, whereas American studies favor experiential assessments. As a result, there is virtually no overlap in the content of the two reports. The happiness section of the Stiglitz-Sen-Fitoussi Report centers on evaluative measures of well-being. By contrast, the psychologists' report explicitly omits these measures and chooses instead to focus on experiential well-being.

The choice of measure is fundamentally important, because it shapes the outcome, leading to conclusions that are not only markedly different but sometimes entirely opposite. As illustration, let me give two examples. The first is the comparative standings of Denmark and Rwanda on the two measures, evaluative and experiential, according to Gallup World Poll data published in the 2012 *World Happiness Report.* On the evaluative gauge, which views a person's life as a whole, Denmark is at the very top of the list, and Rwanda is close to the bottom in a survey of 150 countries. By contrast, on the experiential measure, which asks about happiness yesterday, the two countries have identical scores and rank about 100th out of the 150 countries.

It's easy to understand the difference between the two countries' responses to the *evaluative* question from our discussions about the principal sources of happiness, because it reflects how well governments are addressing people's concerns about their personal happiness. Denmark, a world leader in initiating welfare measures as early as the nineteenth century, is a well-established welfare state; conversely, Rwanda is an emerging nation with a minimal safety net. It's much more difficult to figure out the reason for the virtually identical answers to the *experiential* question about happiness yesterday. Maybe weather conditions were the same and produced similar moods? Perhaps there are genetic/personality similarities between Danes and Rwandans that explain the like responses? At this point, no one knows. The difference between the two countries in responses to the evaluative question makes sense. The same can't be said for the answers to the experiential query.

A second illustration of how evaluative and experiential measures lead to different conclusions is in the treatment of unemployment. The Stiglitz-Sen-Fitoussi Report states that "One aspect where *all research on subjective well-being* does agree concerns the high human costs associated with unemployment" (p. 149, emphasis added). The report details unemployment's effect on evaluative happiness at length and, correspondingly, underscores the need for employment-sustaining policies. This accords with our earlier conclusion about the devastating impact on happiness of massive unemployment in countries transitioning from socialism to capitalism (Chaps. 7 and 8).

In contrast, the psychologists' report devotes a mere 11 *lines* to unemployment toward the end of a *15-page chapter* on public policy (p. 100). Much of the content of the chapter is, frankly, not about policy, but about the need for new and better measures of well-being. Elsewhere, the report minimizes the importance of unemployment, suggesting that "Even a large increase in unemployment, such as experienced in the great recession, may have a muted impact [on happiness]" (p. 72).

"So, on the two types of measures," interjects Ada, who has been quiet to this point, "you seem to be saying that the evaluative is better."

Well, if we want to learn how to increase people's happiness, the evaluative measure favored by economists offers an answer: improve people's life circumstances via job security and safety net policies. The psychologists' measure of experiential happiness, by contrast, doesn't lead to such practical conclusions, and its policy implications, if any, are unclear. Psychologists generally place personality, a fixed characteristic, at the center of happiness analysis, and to the extent that they adopt the experiential measure of temporary moods as guide, they offer little room for interventions to improve happiness.

Ultimately, then, these two measures diverge substantially in what they offer for making personal or public policy decisions to improve happiness. Knowing how life circumstances affect happiness gives us guidance on both the personal and the policy levels. It guides individuals as they make major life decisions, such as choosing between making more money or spending more time at home with one's family. Furthermore, it guides government in its choice between policies that promote economic growth and those that aim to maintain full employment. By comparison, what does the association of experiential measures with personality tell us about how to improve happiness?

"But the psychologists do use both types of measure," insists Ada, "evaluative as well as experiential."

Yes, they do. But there are also differences in evaluative measures, and the two disciplines mostly don't use the same type. Economists typically opt for single-item measures, while psychologists go for multi-item evaluative measures.

"What does that mean?" says Ada.

Well, as you may already have guessed, a single-item measure is the response to a single question. A multi-item measure, by contrast, is an average or some combination of responses to a set of statements or questions.

Economists incline toward single-item measures, because the interpretation is straightforward: You ask how happy a person is, all things considered, and voila! That's what you get in response. Very cut and dried. Psychologists prefer a multi-item measure that solicits responses to a battery of statements or questions. In effect, they believe a shotgun approach is more likely to hit the well-being target. The problem with a multi-item measure, however, is its fuzziness, because each sentence in a multi-item measure inevitably means something different from its predecessor or successor.

A popular happiness measure in psychology, the 5-item Diener Satisfaction With Life Scale, illustrates the ambiguity of multi-item measures. Take a look first at the Diener Scale (Table 13.1).

Now, let's conduct another thought experiment. Imagine a very successful businesswoman, aged 65, who has recently been diagnosed with a life-threatening disease and is now quite ill and bedridden. What would her likely answers to the Diener measure be? Consider just two of the five questions in Table 13.1. In answering question two ("the conditions of my life are excellent"), she would most likely disagree, choosing a numerical value toward the lower end of the 1–7 scale that reflects her failing health. But in answering

Table 13.1 Diener satisfaction with life scale (Handout #8)

Below are five statements with which you may agree or disagree. Indicate your agreement with each item using a 1–7 scale, where 1 = strongly disagree, 2 = disagree, 3 = slightly disagree, 4 = neither agree nor disagree, 5 = slightly agree, 6 = agree, and 7 = strongly agree
1. In most ways, my life is close to my ideal
2. The conditions of my life are excellent
3. I am satisfied with my life
4. So far, I have gotten the important things I want in life
5. If I could live my life over, I would change almost nothing

question five ("if I could live my life over, I would change almost nothing") she is likely to agree, picking a number toward the upper end of the scale that mirrors her successful career.

Why do her answers differ so substantially? Because the two statements have different time frames. Question two is present tense, eliciting information about satisfaction with her current situation, whereas question five is about the past, asking how she feels about her life history. Rather predictably, she is very unhappy with her current situation, but she feels good about her earlier life. When averaged or otherwise combined to get a multi-item response, the two answers offset one another, thus yielding an ambiguous value toward the middle of the agree-disagree distribution. The result, then, is neither indicative of the businesswoman's satisfaction with her current situation nor her life experience.

By contrast, suppose she were presented with the single-item question about life satisfaction, one commonly used in economic research (Chap. 2): "All things considered, how satisfied are you with your life nowadays?" Given her ill health, the response would doubtlessly be toward the lower end of the 1–10 scale. The answer is telling us unambiguously how she feels *at the present time*, that is, how satisfied she is with her life *nowadays*. Similarly, a single-item question like question five of the Diener scale would yield an evaluation of her past life.

Because of the fuzziness of multi-item measures, it would seem that the advantage on this measurement issue goes to economics.

"OK," says Ada resignedly, "I guess economics wins."

On gauging happiness, perhaps, but let's not forget psychology's contribution to vetting happiness. There, psychology wins!

13.4   Methods: More or Less

"OK, but like, this is probably a stupid question," challenges Nancy Ann. "I'm a film and theatre major, so I don't have any idea how you design these happiness studies."

Nancy Ann's asking about method—never a stupid thing! A good question with a lot of bearing on the differences between outcomes in psychology and economics.

For centuries, generalizations about happiness were based not on evidence but on a priori notions of what makes for the good life. As happiness study has moved into the social sciences, evidence-based generalizations have become de rigueur. And yes, evidence is definitely more than a nice thing, because it provides a touchstone, a substantial basis for agreement or disputation. A necessary thing! But what constitutes acceptable evidence? Here, the notion of legitimate evidence differs markedly between psychology and economics.

Both disciplines seek to obtain empirical knowledge based on data from a sample of the population. Economists typically use nationally representative samples in their research, and the generalizations in this volume, on the whole, are based on such samples. Here's the thinking behind such an approach. If we want to deduce useful lessons about happiness, we need research based on a sample that duplicates the characteristics of the country's population as a whole. Such a representative sample matches the composition of the nation's population by gender, age, race, education, income, and so on. Surprisingly, such samples can be as small as 1000 persons, sometimes even less, and still accurately reflect the general population.

In psychology, nationally representative samples comprise only a small part of what generally constitutes acceptable evidence. The common approach is that of psychologist Tim Kasser in his book *The High Price of Materialism* (2002). Kasser bases his findings in the book primarily on a sample of American college students, who, in his words, "second to white rats, form the backbone of much scientific research in psychology" (p. 7). In truth, such samples are usually not even representative of American college students as a whole, because the respondents' colleges are often highly selective research universities, potentially skewing results by education, class, and other factors. What's more, the sample may not even be representative of students at research universities, because the students in the studies have selected themselves into the researcher's psychology class.

"OK, but excuse me," interrupts Nancy Ann, "Prof. Easterlin, you used anecdotal examples in some of our earlier meetings."

True, I have cited the reports of my own students at various points, but only as a close-to-home illustration that supports results from a broader, nationally representative sample.

And now it's my turn to ask the class a question.

"Here's another methodological problem for you. Let's suppose Lily wants to find out whether happiness changes as you go through life. She finds a survey conducted in the year 2000 and puts the average happiness response for each 5-year age group in order from ages 20–24 up to ages 70–74. She notes that the oldest age group is significantly happier than the youngest. Can she safely infer from this point-of-time comparison that as they age people tend to be happier in their early 70s than in their early 20s?"

"I know!" Emma bursts out. "She can't, because these are different people. The 70–74-year-olds are not the same people as the 20–24-year-olds. You need to study the *same* people at different ages, if what you want is to see how their happiness changes over the life cycle. In your question, Lily is using cross-section data, and the members of each age group are different people!"

Exactly right, Emma. Those ages 20–24 in the year 2000 were born in 1976–1980; those 70–74 were born way back in 1926–1930. So, they are from different birth cohorts, and they have different life histories. Just to take one example, if we compare the two cohorts when they were in their 20s, those in the younger cohort were much less likely to be married than those in the older. In itself, this marriage difference would make the younger cohort less happy at ages 20–24. Definitely, it would be mistaken to assume on the basis of cross-section data that the happiness of today's 20–24-year-olds tells us anything at all about the happiness of the older cohort when they were that age. In short, linking together those currently aged 20–24 and 70–74 will not give us a correct picture of the life cycle happiness of *either* birth cohort.

Unfortunately, cross-section research like this, with a few notable exceptions, is the almost universal practice in psychology. One dubious result is that psychologists, for the most part, judge the explanatory importance of variables from such point-of-time results. For example, in cross-section analysis, personality and personality-related variables like religion frequently play a much larger role in explaining happiness differences among individuals than do life circumstances such as income or health. Because of this cross-section result, psychologists are apt to downplay the importance of life circumstances as determinants of happiness and instead favor setpoint theory. But over time, personality variables change very little, while life circumstances vary considerably; so, the life course of happiness is chiefly shaped by life circumstances (Chap. 10). As we've seen repeatedly, point-of-time data can be very misleading in telling us what actually happens to happiness over time, and this is a good example.

On the whole, economists are more sensitive to the difference between cross-section and time-series research. They usually draw a sharp distinction between the two and engage in relatively more time-series studies. However, they are not immune to predicting time-series change based on cross-section findings, as we'll see in the next lesson's discussion of the threshold concept.

"Well," concludes Ada, "Economics can't always be right, but you do make some good points about choosing samples, considering time frames, and things like that. It seems pretty much like economics is getting some better results."

"At least," she smiles, "for studying happiness."

13.5 Do We Have a Winner?

No, certainly not. Economics has an advantage on some methodological issues, but not all of them. It is woefully deficient, for example, in checking on the reliability and validity of happiness measures. Psychology definitely pays more attention to what people say and recognizes the importance of internal benchmarks in forming personal judgments. Truth be told, in the final analysis, when it comes to explaining happiness, work in both disciplines is essential. It is not a matter of whether economics or psychology is right.

Happiness is truly an interdisciplinary subject.

References and Further Reading

Akerlof, G. A. (2020). Sins of omission and the practice of economics. *Journal of Economic Literature, 58*(2), 405–418.

Diener, E., & Lucas, R. E. (1999). Personality and subjective well-being. In D. Kahneman, E. Diener, & N. Schwarz (Eds.), *Well-being: The foundations of hedonic psychology* (pp. 213–229). New York: Russell Sage Foundation.

Kasser, T. (2002). *The high price of materialism*. Cambridge, MA: MIT Press.

Lucas, R. E., Clark, A. E., Georgellis, Y., & Diener, E. (2004). Unemployment alters the set point for life satisfaction. *Psychological Science, 15*(1), 8–13.

Pigou, A. C. (1932). *The economics of welfare*. London, UK: Macmillan.

Stiglitz, J., Sen, A., & Fitoussi, J. P. (2009). Report by the commission on the measurement of economic performance and social progress. Available at www.stiglitz-sen-fitoussi.fr

Thaler, R. H. (2015). *Misbehaving: The making of behavioral economics*. New York: W. W. Norton.

United States National Research Council. (2013). *Subjective well-being: Measuring happiness, suffering, and other dimensions of human experience*. Washington, DC: The National Academies Press.

14

Critiquing the Paradox

14.1   How About Really Poor Countries?

"I read somewhere that the Paradox applies only above a certain threshold," Larry announces, frowning, "above some minimum level of per capita GDP, and that in those countries where most people are really poor more money makes them happier. That makes sense to me, and there's evidence for it."

A very helpful comment, especially because this view of the Paradox is not only common but even voiced by some happiness scholars. It's particularly popular among advocates of economic growth. Discerning a threshold below which the Paradox seemingly does not apply, they can say, "Look! Growth does improve happiness when incomes are low. It's only in countries where income is already plenty high that the Paradox applies. The argument that economic growth doesn't increase happiness just pertains to affluent countries."

But they're wrong. The Paradox holds in countries across the board: rich, poor, and in between. Sure, as Larry claims, there are data to support the threshold theory—but by now, all of you can predict the method that's producing the questionable result. You guessed it! This is yet another case of cross-section evidence providing the presumptive supporting data and leading, yet again, to a mistaken conclusion.

If you plot statistics for happiness and GDP per capita *at a given point in time* for countries worldwide, a curve fitted to the data looks like that in Fig. 14.1. And what do we see? When incomes are low, greater happiness coincides with higher income. Eventually, however, as income reaches relatively high levels, happiness levels off. The threshold notion of the Paradox relies on this picture, which shows the Paradox kicking in only after a country

© The Author(s), under exclusive license to Springer Nature Switzerland AG 2021
R. A. Easterlin, *An Economist's Lessons on Happiness*,
https://doi.org/10.1007/978-3-030-61962-6_14

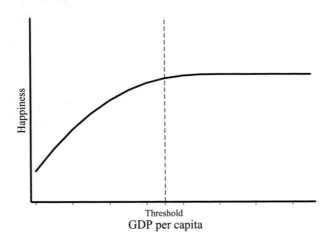

Fig. 14.1 Regression line fitted to international cross section of happiness and real GDP per capita (Handout #9)

reaches some reasonably high level of GDP per capita—the *threshold*. Above the threshold, there is no further boost in happiness as income goes up. Consistent with this comparison among nations, cross-section data for persons within a given country paint a picture similar to Fig. 14.1. In a recent analysis of US statistics, the threshold has actually been set at a yearly income of $75,000.

Among low-income countries (*left side* of threshold), those with higher GDP per capita tend to be happier; among high-income countries (*right side* of threshold), there is little difference in happiness as GDP per capita gets bigger.

According to the threshold view, then, a low-income country whose income is growing over time should follow the upward sloping segment of the curve depicting increasing happiness (at the left end of Fig. 14.1). But does that happen—does the cross-section evidence capture the actual historical experience of low-income countries?

By now, you all know where I'm going to look for the answer. (Larry is shaking his head.)

"Yep, we know!"

Let's consider the time-series data for three countries which start from quite low-income levels but have had in recent times a growth rate of per capita GDP that is the highest or close to the highest ever in the world. The first is China from 1990 to 2015, whose phenomenal growth experience we discussed in detail (Chap. 7). The second is Japan from 1958 to 1987. Compared to the United States in 1987, Japan started with an income about one-eighth as large; by 1987, it was up to two-thirds as great. At the start of this period, hardly any Japanese owned electric washing machines or refrigerators, but by the end, these appliances were well-nigh universal. In the same time span, car ownership soared from 1 to 60% of households. The third country is India in the quarter century from 1995 to 2019. During this period, real GDP per capita more than quadrupled; in the previous *half* century, real GDP per capita failed even to double. Admittedly, the reliability of the recent data on India is somewhat uncertain; nevertheless, the rate of economic growth accelerated markedly post-1995. About that, there's no doubt.

If there are any countries where economic growth raises happiness before reaching the threshold, as predicted by Fig. 14.1, surely these countries should be the ones.

So, did any of the three countries in fact follow the upward sloping curve of Fig. 14.1? The answer is, emphatically, "no." Despite a demonstrable advance in living levels, happiness failed to increase in all three (see Fig. 14.2). Indeed, in India, the trend is downward. Note that there is no indication of a threshold in any of the countries. As is often the case, the cross section does not predict the time series.

The lesson repeats itself.

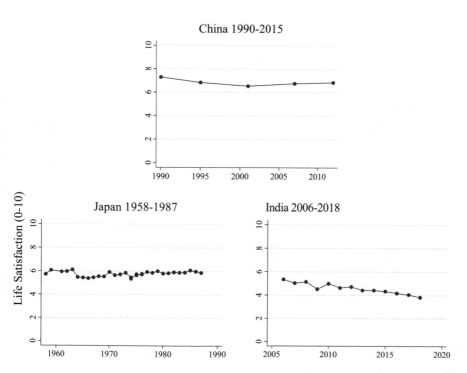

Fig. 14.2 Happiness in three formerly poor countries during subsequent periods of very rapid economic growth (Handout # 10)

The response scale for Japan is 1–4 but was converted to 0–10 for comparable presentation. Cantril Ladder data are presented for India. Source: China, World Values Survey; Japan, World Database of Happiness; India, Gallup World Poll.

Contrary to the cross-section data, the time-series evidence demonstrates that the Paradox holds in low- as well as high-income countries. Greater happiness does not accompany an upward trend in income, even a very steep one, as in these three formerly poor countries. The message of the data is irrefutable: *Economic growth in itself does not increase happiness.* Social comparison is at work everywhere. Even in low-income countries, social comparison undermines the expected positive effect on happiness of higher income—that's certainly reflected in the experience of Japan, China, and India. As incomes rise overall, even from very low levels, so too do people's notions of what constitutes the good life. The result: no improvement in happiness, even though people's material conditions are considerably better.

The standard for satisfaction has shifted effortlessly. In the media, evidence abounds for the ubiquity of social comparison. Flipping through old news reports, the eye lands on items like these:

New York Times, September 22, 2006:
  In China, Children of the Rich Learn Class, Minus the Struggle.
  "…. In addition to early golf training, which has become wildly popular, affluent parents are enrolling their children in everything from ballet and private music lessons, to classes in horse riding, ice skating, skiing, and even polo."
  Orange County Register, August 27, 2013:
  China's Orange County Represents a Lifestyle.
  "An hour's drive north of Beijing… sits Orange County, China … a 143-unit housing development designed to resemble neighborhoods that are 6,000 miles away in Southern California…. 'People in the United States may think of Orange County as a place,' said [developer] Zhang Bo…. But in China, people feel Orange County is a brand name, something like Giorgio Armani. It's a kind of people's new lifestyle. It's fresh. It's more like rising, improving, excitement.'"
  New York Times, March 19, 2010:
  For India's Newly Rich Farmers, Limos Won't Do.
  "'Everyone wants to be better than the others,' said Subhash Goyal, whose travel company handles three or four helicopter weddings every year…. 'This is how the new rich behave. They want to show off and say, 'I have more money than you.'"

As incomes rise generally, even from very low levels, so too do people's notions of what constitutes the good life: You've got it by now—their income reference levels increase. They've got more, but they also want more. The result is no improvement in happiness, even though their material conditions are considerably better. As far as income is concerned, Samuel Johnson, writing over two centuries ago, hit the nail on the head: "Life is a progression from want to want, not from enjoyment to enjoyment."

14.2 Why Are Richer Countries Happier?

Larry is not about to give up. He points at Fig. 14.1.

"Well, if it's not economic growth, then how did the high-income countries get to be happier than the low-income countries? To me, that graph shows that raising the income of poorer countries increases happiness. Isn't that what it shows?"

Excellent question, Larry. It puts you in the best of company. The argument you're making— the greater happiness of higher-income countries proves that economic growth boosts happiness—has also been put forward by, among others, two Nobel Prize winners in economics.

But let's remember a basic principle of logical analysis: *that correlation does not mean causation.* You're assuming that the positive cross-section association between income and happiness means that there is necessarily a causal connection running from income to happiness. It overlooks the possibility that other causes might be at work.

"Such as?" Larry asks.

"I know!" says Ada. "It's the welfare state."

That's right, Ada, we've already seen the answer to this—happiness increases with the scope and generosity of welfare state programs (Chap. 8). These government policies and programs are responsible for the greater happiness of richer countries.

Larry doesn't look convinced.

OK, so let me dig up some additional evidence. Here we go. Cross-section studies of around 40 OECD member countries have found that happiness is higher in the countries that have stronger safety nets. For example, people are happier in countries where unemployment benefits relative to wages are higher than in countries where the ratio is lower, other things constant. Again, data for Latin American countries reveal that social assistance programs, such as cash transfers to those in poverty, are positively associated with happiness.

Kelsey J. O'Connor, whom you've already met (Fig. 10.2), has extended this type of analysis to countries worldwide. He found a positive cross-section association between happiness and welfare state policies in data for well over

100 countries. When he subdivided the countries into three groups—developed, in transition, and less developed—the positive relation repeated itself in each category.

Recent time-series data also accord with the positive relationship between safety net policies and happiness. In most Latin American countries, happiness increased noticeably from the two decades before to the two decades after the turn of the century. In country after country, a shift to governments whose policies focused on job creation and a social safety net was associated with increased happiness. In the 1980s and 1990s, the so-called Washington Consensus, a set of policies that emphasized fiscal discipline (avoiding government budget deficits) and debt repayment to other countries, put Latin American countries through the wringer. Unemployment rates were high and social spending low. Then, in the early 2000s, a shift to more welfare-oriented governments swept across much of Latin America. Happiness increased significantly, especially in the countries that achieved the lowest unemployment rates and had the highest social spending. In contrast, differences among countries in the rate of economic growth, as indexed by GDP per capita, bore no relation to the trends in happiness. It was the shift to policies focusing on employment and the safety net that did the job.

Some analysts think the Paradox implies that public policy can do little to help low-income countries. That's wrong. The Paradox tells us that economic growth in itself will not make people happier. But social policies can. Rather than a primary focus on raising GDP, the emphasis should be on employment and the social safety net. There is no better example than the case of China in the 1990s (Chap. 7). Even though GDP per capita increased dramatically, happiness declined as employment went south and the social safety net unraveled. Once the government reversed these policies, happiness turned upward.

Lily comes to Larry's aid.

"But look, professor," she says, "The countries with the best welfare state policies are the richer ones. That shows that high income's necessary, right, for countries to afford safety net policies? So, the economic growth people are probably right. There's just an added causal link. Add 'welfare state policy' to the chain. It's not just 'economic growth leads to greater happiness'; it's 'economic growth leads to welfare state policy and welfare state policy leads to greater happiness.' Economic growth really is the main source of higher happiness."

That's good reasoning, Lily. But let me ask you this: If welfare state policies are simply a normal product of economic growth, then shouldn't time-series statistics show happiness increasing in *all countries* when income grows, and the greater the growth in income, the more the increase in happiness? The actual time-series evidence, however, indicates that happiness and economic growth *do not* automatically go together.

Moreover, welfare state policies can be implemented at low levels of GDP per capita, even with little or no economic growth. As we saw, the welfare state of Costa Rica, with a GDP per capita one-fourth of that in the United States, is one of the happiest countries in the world (Chap. 8).

Sure, generally speaking, welfare state policies are most advanced in richer countries. But let's remember again that correlation doesn't imply causation. In fact, the sources of these countries' wealth, on the one hand, and their happiness, on the other, aren't the same. The high-income countries are *rich* because they were the leaders in adopting the new technology of the Industrial Revolution, itself the product of breakthroughs in the natural sciences. The high-income countries are *happy* because they were the pioneers in developing the social science knowledge leading to the formulation of welfare state policies. Thus, at a given point in time, the same countries are usually high on both income per capita and welfare state policies. But one didn't cause the other; instead, the same countries were the first to reap the benefits of two new and different fields of scientific knowledge—one, the natural sciences, underlying modern economic growth, and, the other, the social sciences, responsible for policies to advance human well-being. (We'll learn more about this very soon [Chap. 16].) The diagram does not reflect a causal relation between income and happiness. It is simply telling us that the leaders and laggards were the same in the occurrence of modern economic growth and in the adoption of welfare state policies.

In short, richer countries are happier because of their employment and safety net policies, not economic growth. Economic growth is not prerequisite to these policies, which governments can introduce at relatively low levels of income. The higher-income countries are both rich and happy because they were the leaders in developing the differing domains of scientific knowledge underlying both greater material wealth and welfare state policies.

14.3 How Much Time Is in a Time Series?

"So I just Googled 'Easterlin Paradox—Criticisms,' and found an article called 'Debunking the Easterlin Paradox,' Jill announces. "Man, it's pretty harsh. Have you seen it?"

Yes, I've seen it. And indeed, the authors are the most relentless critics of the Paradox by far. Here I've been praising the worth of time-series studies, and what do they find? A time series that's out of sync with my findings.

The question is this, then: "Why do some time-series studies show a positive relation between income and happiness, not the nil relation in the Paradox?" Well, because there's actually not much *time* in those particular series! Briefly put, the time series in the analysis is too short to identify trends, and short series yield the *short-term* positive association between happiness and income due to the concurrent fluctuations in the two series. The Paradox, in contrast, is about the relationship between the *long-term trends* in happiness and income, and this association is nil.

Let's go back to the early discussion in which we distinguished between the short- and long-run time-series relations of happiness and income. Remember this figure from our third class? (Fig. 14.3). In the short run, the two series move up and down together, but in the long run, there is no relationship. The short run reflects the positive association of fluctuations in the two series, whereas the long run highlights the nil relation of the trends.

In the short term, happiness and income go up and down together (solid lines), but in the long term, the trend in happiness does not correspond with the trend in income (broken lines).

Clearly, in order to test the Paradox, what we want are the trends in happiness and income, and to get at the trends, you need time series for each country that are as long as possible. If your series are short, you are likely to end up with a result reflecting the short-run fluctuations. The article challenging the Paradox that Jill pulled up on her laptop draws on two data sets, the World Values Survey (WVS) and the Eurobarometer. In both cases, the authors make decisions that shorten the time series they analyze considerably, so much so that the end result is the positive short-run relationship due to the concurrent fluctuations in the two series.

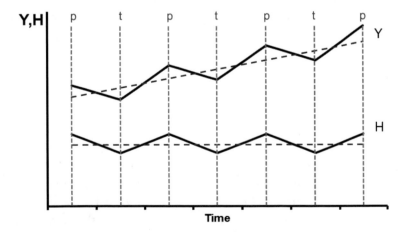

Fig. 14.3 Short-term fluctuations and long-term trends in happiness and income: An illustration

In regard to the World Values Survey (WVS), the authors analyze data from waves two and four, surveys that were conducted respectively around the beginning and end of the 1990s. Inexplicably, the authors chose not to include data from wave five, although those data were available to them 4 years before the article's publication. Including wave five would have added 5–7 years to the length of the series they were studying. By omitting wave five, they end up with series about a decade or less long and with a statistical result dominated by the positive association due to short-term fluctuations.

Their Eurobarometer analysis repeats this story. The Eurobarometer is a semi-annual survey that started in the early 1970s with about nine European countries. Over time, the country coverage has gradually expanded. Although the data for some countries span as much as 30 years or more, the authors of this article subdivide the series for all countries into 10-year segments. As with the exclusion of wave five of the WVS, the outcome is a much briefer time series and a result reflecting the positive short-run association (though in this case one that is not even statistically significant).

In their treatment of the data in both the WVS and Eurobarometer studies, then, the authors of Jill's article made decisions that went in the wrong direction, shortening the series and ending with the positive association between the fluctuations in happiness and GDP. They gave the Paradox the short end of the stick! To test for the Paradox, we clearly want time series that are longer than 10 years in length.

But how many years are needed to identify the long-term trend? There was a time when I thought I could venture an answer, but that time is long gone. What changed my mind was the data on happiness for many of the transition countries.

As we saw, the transition from socialism to capitalism involves an initial precipitous economic collapse and subsequent slow recovery (Chap. 7). Happiness follows suit; indeed, even now—two decades into the twenty-first century—happiness in the transition countries is probably still below its level 5–10 years before the transition.

Unfortunately, happiness data for many transition countries began to be collected only after the period of economic collapse. Thus, for these countries, happiness statistics to go with those for GDP exist just for the period of economic recovery, a period in some countries now of about two or more decades in length. If we fit trend lines to the happiness and GDP series for these countries, they'll draw exactly the short-run positive association of happiness and income during the long, slow economic recovery, not the nil or zero relation evidenced by countries like Russia for which the happiness data reach back into the period before the economic collapse. Thus, as a number of the transition countries illustrate, even 20 years may not be long enough to identify trends.

"Yeah, but I want to get back to the comment I Googled. Here's what it says, Prof. Easterlin—that what you do is a 'mishmash of statistics.' That's pretty mean, isn't it?"

Sure, Jill—I'd hope, first, that anyone really interested would go back to read my original article. And ordinarily, I prefer to keep my personal feelings out of the discussion. (But I can see that a number of students are on the edge of their seats, some thinking twice about a future life as a scholar.) So … well, yes—of course. Even a social scientist finds such remarks disturbing. It's unfortunate in academic discourse when analysts stoop to pejoratives as a substitute for reason. In the pursuit of knowledge, there's always back and forth—this is how progress is made. But there's no reason for incivility, and many good reasons to avoid it.

There's a better approach to scholarly debate, eloquently expressed some six centuries ago by Leonardo Bruni in a letter to Thomas Cambiatore:

> If your letter had praised everything of mine, I would not be as pleased as I am by your attempt to disprove and reject certain points. I regard this as a mark of friendship and the other as one of adulation. But in return I ask you to listen with an open mind to my rebuttal. For what you say, if it were allowed to pass without any reply from me, would be too one-sided. (As quoted in Griffiths 2003, 352)

To my mind, this sets the standard for intellectual exchange. The continuing debate I have had with one of the great pioneers of happiness research, Dutch sociologist Ruut Veenhoven, aspires to this standard (Fig. 14.4). Over

Fig. 14.4 A happy sociologist: Ruut Veenhoven (Courtesy of Ruut Veenhoven)

the years, Ruut has been an incessant critic of the Paradox, and I have sought to reply in kind. I like to think that the tone of our exchanges matches that of Bruni and Cambiatore and that, most important of all, the progress of knowledge benefits from such polite dissent.

Ruut and I are all the better for our cordial debates—and happier, with no money spent.

14.4 Time's Up

Here's the gist. Critics of the Paradox present evidence of a positive association between happiness and income based on either of two statistical relationships—the cross-section correlation or the short-run time-series linkage between fluctuations in happiness and income. The Paradox, however, is about a third association, that between *long-run trends* in happiness and income, and the long-run relationship is nil.

The Paradox is manifest in the long-run trend.

References and Further Reading

Easterlin, R. A. (2017). Paradox lost? *Review of Behavioral Economics, 4*(4), 311–339.

Griffiths, G. (2003). Letter from Bruni to Thomas Cambiatore. *Journal of European Economic History, 32*(2), 352–359.

O'Connor, K. J. (2017). Happiness and welfare state policy around the world. *Review of Behavioral Economics, 4*(4), 397–420.

Part IV

History Lessons

15

Dawn of the Happiness Revolution

15.1   Labor Pains and Birthday Greetings

"Happiness studies seem kind of outside of economics. I mean, before I saw the course listings, I never knew economists studied or taught that sort of thing. So," Andy asks, hesitating, "What did economists think when you came up with the Paradox?"

To be honest, Andy, this is hardly my favorite topic. No bright balloons launched at its birth: The Paradox fell completely flat. I thought my article presenting the Paradox was pretty good—it was the first to use happiness data, and it presented an unexpected outcome, because people just automatically assume that more money brings greater happiness. But the article was immediately rejected by the *American Economic Review*, the discipline's lead journal, with a brief note: "Nothing new here."

Honestly, I shouldn't have been surprised. While in retrospect the Paradox marked the start of a new field, dubbed the economics of happiness, at that time happiness, as a subject of study, was anathema to most of the profession.

"But why weren't economists excited?!", bursts out Lily. "When you do that sort of study, you know, the data lead to new ideas. That's a good thing, isn't it? I thought that's what universities are for."

Yes, new ideas are a good thing—not all will pan out, of course, but the valid ones usually stick in the long run. Knowledge emerges slowly over the course of time, and that's only possible with new ideas. But Andy's question reflects the fact that that we all have preconceptions—in this case about the scope of a discipline—and preconceptions govern academic disciplines as much as they do everything else. Every field of study operates within a set of

R. A. Easterlin, *An Economist's Lessons on Happiness*,
https://doi.org/10.1007/978-3-030-61962-6_15

generally agreed-upon assumptions, called the disciplinary "paradigm," which Thomas Kuhn pointed out in regard to the natural sciences in his classic 1962 study *The Structure of Scientific Revolutions*. In scholarship, the paradigm moves a field forward but also sets parameters. The paradigm effect holds, whether we're looking at the theoretical foundations of a discipline or its methodological protocols.

None of this is as esoteric as it sounds, so let me see elaborate a bit.

When I produced my first results on happiness, the discipline was in a behaviorist strait-jacket. Behaviorism means focusing exclusively on people's observable behavior. (Warning: Be careful here about terminology—don't confuse behaviorism, a psychological concept, with behavioral economics; the two are frankly at opposite ends of the spectrum.) Behaviorism in the social sciences was profoundly influenced by the psychologist B.F. Skinner, who reacted against efforts to understand internal cognition and mental traits of humans. Skinner reverted to the Lockean notion of the tabula rasa, the mind as a blank slate. To the economist who subscribes to behaviorism, what people say about their desires, their feelings, and the motivations for their behavior—self-reports or subjective testimony—is summarily rejected as legitimate evidence. In the proud words of Victor Fuchs, one-time president of the American Economic Association:

> Economists, as a rule, are not concerned with the internal thought processes of the decision-maker or in the rationalizations the decision-maker offers to explain his or her behavior. Economists believe that what people *do* is more relevant than what they say. (Fuchs, 1983, 14, emphasis in original)

Here's an example of the limit this paradigm in economics sets. Imagine you were asked, "If you could choose exactly the number of children to have in your whole life, how many would that be?" Would you believe that your answer, along with that of other respondents, would be dismissed as worthless by economists trying to explain child-bearing behavior? Hard to believe. Yet such was the case in the economics of the 1970s.

Economists' contempt for subjective testimony flames forth in Fuchs' use of the pejorative word "rationalizations" for a person's explanation of her or his behavior. In his view, individuals aren't even credited with having valid reasons. It's as though people passively watch their own lives, like the audience of a play, and their reasons for their decisions and actions are tantamount to speculations about Hamlet's motives. But unlike surmises about the motives of fictional characters, the actual explanations of real humans for their behavior are, in fact, highly informative.

Fortunately, a few economists were becoming restive in Fuchs' time, as illustrated by economic historian Deidre McCloskey's sardonic description of a typical economics student-faculty workshop:

> Unlike other social sciences, economists are extremely hostile toward question-naires and other self-descriptions.... One can literally get an audience of economists to laugh out loud by proposing ironically to send out a questionnaire on some disputed economic point. Economists.... are unthinkingly committed to the notion that only the externally observable behavior of actors is admissible evidence in arguments concerning economics. (McCloskey 1983, 514)

To put it baldly, according to mainstream economics, the Paradox, in crediting what people say about their happiness, lost sight of the rules of discipline. I had violated a sacred precept: Economists do not listen to what people say.

"Excuse me, professor," says Ada, obviously excited, "We learned how ridiculous this is in my neuroscience seminar—how wrong the blank slate is. People not only think, have internal processes, but emotional processes coming from the body and mind together influence so-called reason. It's called embodied mind now!" she announces proudly.

Well, Ada, I'm sure you're the expert on this one, but 50 years ago, no economist wanted to hear it.

What's more, paying attention to subjective testimony was not the only perceived problem with the Paradox. In combining the responses of different individuals to compute a country's average happiness, the Paradox implicitly assumes that different individuals have approximately the same scale of happiness and that, therefore, we can reliably compare groups. This assumption broke with another mainstay of the discipline's paradigm—its stance on comparing persons. In the 1930s, Lionel Robbins of the London School of Economics had pronounced on purely deductive grounds that "interpersonal comparisons of utility [=happiness] could not be made." Suppose, for example, that a person with an annual income of $100,000 transfers $1000 to a person whose income is $5000. Although most of us would say that the loss of well-being experienced by the richer person is negligible, while the gain in well-being of the poorer person is substantial, Robbins said, "No. We cannot measure well-being, and therefore cannot compare the effects of the transfer on the two persons." In Robbins' view, economics couldn't be considered a legitimate science if it were to embark on such judgments, because they honor people's subjective feelings.

Fearing a threat to the scientific respectability of the discipline, economics, on the whole, accepted Robbins' view and stuck to it faithfully for decades. Unwittingly, in the case of the Paradox, I took a different approach, influenced no doubt by my prior immersion in demography, a discipline that did listen to what people said about the reasons for their behavior. So, when I came across Hadley Cantril's survey results, demonstrating the commonality in people's basic concerns around the world, they made sense to me and seemed to justify interpersonal comparisons at the group level (Chap. 2). Moreover, the open-ended nature of Cantril's interviews, which did not steer people toward certain answers like a multiple-choice questionnaire did, reinforced my confidence in his approach. Asked simply to speak their minds, people came up with remarkably similar sources of happiness. But because of an established precept, a part of the paradigm that rejected interpersonal comparisons, the discipline dismissed the Paradox rather than delve into a new and surprising result.

And then, the main message of the Paradox—that economic growth does *not* improve the human lot—ran against the grain. A basic conclusion of economic theory is that greater well-being goes with higher income. Economists by and large have exhibited steadfast allegiance to this principle, as evidenced by a rapporteur's write-up of a workshop discussion in 2008. According to this report, Nobel Laureate in economics Robert Barro proclaims that "if the [empirical] results indicated … [that higher income doesn't register greater well-being], he would conclude that either the data or methods were flawed in some way, not that there is no relation between happiness and income" [*Brookings Papers on Economic Activity*, Spring 2008, p. 101.]. This, from a specialist in econometrics, an empirically oriented subfield of economics!

The conclusion of my study, that increases in income and well-being do not go hand-in-hand, contradicted this seemingly self-evident principle. It's sort of like the icing off the cake—and thus not a surprise that the Paradox was almost universally rejected or ignored. After all, it was a big cake with a lot of icing—decades of economic research. A lot more than theory is at stake when a foundational assumption is called into question. Most policy proposals emanating from economics focus exclusively on what happens to income, because it assumes that higher income invariably means greater well-being.

Acceptance of subjective testimony, interpersonal comparisons, and a non-existent happiness-income relationship: These were the sins of the Paradox. No wonder it was summarily dismissed by the economics profession at the time of its birth.

"Oh, well!" says Ada, beaming at her student (me!). "You had friends among the psychs."

15.2   Formative Years

"Sounds like a tough road. So, when did people get interested in happiness economics? What changed the attitude?" asks Carolyn.

Cracks in the behaviorist fortress were beginning to show by the 1990s. Leaving people's views out of the equations intended to explain their behavior did not sit well with all economists, including influential figures like Alan Blinder of Princeton University and one-time Federal Reserve Board Governor. Blinder pointed out the absurdity of the behaviorist framework with this memorable gibe: "If molecules could talk, would chemists refuse to listen?"

Labor economics was one of the few sub-disciplines in which some economists did open their ears to what people say—specifically, to what they reported as their job satisfaction. To be sure, it was a jump—and a rather big one at that—from "job" to "life" satisfaction (= happiness). But a few brave souls, led by Andrew Oswald at the University of Warwick in England, made the leap (Fig. 15.1). If the Paradox was the seed planted for the Happiness Revolution, it was Oswald and his successors whose empirical studies nurtured its growth and helped it thrive.

Oswald, together with David Blanchflower of Dartmouth College, was responsible for a key breakthrough in happiness research, the estimation from cross-section data of a *microeconomic happiness equation*. Basically, the equation measures the point-of-time statistical relation between happiness and

Fig. 15.1 Happy economists: Oswald and Author (*left*) (Courtesy of Andrew Oswald)

people's life circumstances—including, among other things, their age, gender, marital status, health, employment status, and, of course, income. The Oswald-Blanchflower work provided a model that a researcher in any country could easily replicate and extend, and so, in the course of time, it found a large number of followers.

In 1997, Oswald published "Happiness and Economic Performance," a paper summarizing a number of results from this new research. The fact that the paper appeared in the *Economic Journal*, the leading British periodical in economics, helped establish the legitimacy of economic research on happiness. Thanks to the work of Oswald and his followers, by the turn of the century, happiness had gained a small but firm foothold in economics.

Economists were beginning to listen to what people had to say.

"Yeah, but why?" asks Carolyn. "What made them pay attention?"

You're right to press on this, Carolyn—paradigms are resistant to change. The Oswald-Blanchflower model was an important methodological stimulus, but a number of other developments contributed to the emergence of happiness economics. First, a growing body of well-vetted happiness data, a veritable gold mine of information on an alluring subject, was now available to all researchers. Concurrently, expanding recognition of psychological influences on economic behavior and a resulting acceptance of what people said about their own lives had taken hold in a new area of economics, behavioral economics, as well as its subfield, behavioral finance. Also, the few economists who had ventured into psychology found that, within that discipline, happiness had become an important field of study, with measures of happiness carefully vetted. Finally, a number of policy-makers and scholars were growing increasingly disillusioned with the ubiquitous measure of a country's well-being—yes, you know it well by now, GDP per capita—and they were searching for a better metric.

"Well," interjects Keaton, "Were there some others working with these ideas? I mean, there probably had to be, for things to change."

Yes, Keaton—it takes a village, doesn't it? In fact, it wasn't economics but other social sciences that produced and accumulated much of the early happiness data. You remember my research colleague and counterpart in scholarly debate, the sociologist Ruut Veenhoven (Fig. 14.4). In Europe in 1984, Ruut published the World Database of Happiness. He and his colleagues assembled, classified, and evaluated happiness surveys from around the world, which was not only an extremely valuable but an enormously arduous undertaking, and he made the results available to researchers everywhere. Around the same time, the American political scientist Ronald Inglehart mobilized scholars, first in Europe and then worldwide, to conduct the European and

World Values Surveys. And in psychology, our early acquaintance here Ed Diener, of the Diener scale, in pioneering research at the University of Illinois was putting happiness on the discipline's map and inspiring psychologists' surveys of subjective well-being (Chap. 13).

Another central development was the field of behavioral economics, which focuses on how people make decisions. Its breakthrough dates to a seminal 1979 article by psychologists Daniel Kahneman (that guy again!) and Amos Tversky, "Prospect Theory: An Analysis of Decision under Risk." Behavioral economics differs from happiness economics in two ways. First and foremost, it analyzes people's decision-making processes, whereas happiness economics explores the results of decisions. For instance, a behavioral economist might investigate how people decide the number of children they will have, but a happiness economist would ask, instead, whether having children makes people happier. In terms of the concepts we've studied, behavioral economics is primarily interested in decision utility—the expected satisfaction resulting from a particular choice—and happiness economics, in experienced utility, the satisfaction actually realized (Chap. 11).

The two fields also differ in methodology. Behavioral economics relies mainly on laboratory experiments of the type developed by and commonly used in social psychology. Happiness economics, by contrast, relies primarily on social survey data.

Because the foremost concern of the discipline of economics is how people make choices—some economists, *a la Pareto*, would say the sole concern (Chap. 11)—behavioral economics has been quicker to gain acceptance than the economics of happiness. Be that as it may, behavioral economics has paved the way for legitimizing happiness economics, because it pays attention to what people say and demonstrates the importance of psychological influences on economic behavior.

Well, like, what about psychology?" asks Nancy Ann, smiling over at Ada. "Did it do a better job?"

"I bet it did!" says Ada.

Certainly, Nancy Ann, we'd hope that would be the case, wouldn't we, in a discipline that studies the human mind. Nevertheless, psychology itself was generally dismissive of happiness research before 1970. Until then, the areas of psychology concerned with moods, feelings, and subjective contentment were focused mainly on people with mental illness. But in the 1970s, thanks particularly to the work of Ed Diener, things began to change. Diener and his collaborators demonstrated that survey data on happiness could provide valuable insights into the psychological well-being of the population as a whole, not just a subset of it, and helped establish *positive psychology*, a new field dedicated to understanding what makes for the emotional health of the ordinary person. Among other things, this body of research, as we saw early on, tested for and confirmed the meaningfulness of data on self-reported happiness (Chap. 2). Its conclusions about the reliability and validity of happiness data were not lost on economists who had become interested in the subject and who repeatedly cited the robust findings of psychologists to demonstrate the worthiness of happiness as a subject deserving serious study in economics.

Finally, in the realm of public policy, happiness economics benefited from a growing disillusionment with per capita GDP as the measure of societal well-being par excellence. As critics of GDP pointed out, there are many other sources of well-being than just people's incomes, and the public policy focus on growth of GDP led to neglect of matters like education and health. What became known as the *social indicators movement*, which put forward a range of societal measures indicating a nation's well-being, was at the forefront of this misgiving about the monolithic importance of GDP. Happiness fit into this new perspective.

15.3   Happiness in Bloom

"O.k., but accepting a theory, that's fine." Tyler's getting impatient. "Don't they need to use these ideas to have a point?"

"He's right, professor!" Keaton pipes up. "Where's the meaningful social change?"

Hold on, guys—we're getting there.

What began in the last three decades of the twentieth century as a shift in philosophy about how to measure and augment human well-being grew after the turn of the century into a viewpoint influencing politics and public awareness. As mentioned earlier, Nicholas Sarkozy, president of France from 2007 to 2012, was notably dissatisfied with per capita GDP as a measure of quality of life, and in February 2008, he asked three economists—Joseph Stiglitz, Amartya Sen (both Nobel Prize winners in economics), and Jean-Paul Fitoussi—to create a commission to consider better ways of measuring social progress. The resulting 25-member group included 22 scholars with advanced degrees in economics, most earned in the economic epoch of behaviorism and, among them, five Nobel prize winners in economics. With so many highly decorated researchers from the discipline in its ranks, the Commission's findings, *The Report of the Commission on the Measurement of Economic Performance and Social Progress* (2009), stood as a major milestone in the acceptance of happiness by economists and opened the door to greater public awareness.

Among the Commission's recommendations in the Report was the forthright endorsement of measures of "subjective well-being," the blanket term used to encompass both the evaluative and momentary mood measures we discussed earlier. The Commission's stance is unequivocal:

> Research has shown that it is possible to collect meaningful and reliable data on subjective as well as objective well-being. Subjective well-being encompasses different aspects (cognitive evaluations of one's life, happiness, satisfaction, positive emotions such as joy and pride, and negative emotions such as pain and worry): each of them should be measured separately to derive a more comprehensive appreciation of people's lives.... [T]he types of questions that have proved their value within small-scale and unofficial surveys should be included in larger-scale surveys undertaken by official statistical offices. (p. 16)

Only 40 years earlier, it would have been unimaginable—indeed, economic heresy—for any prominent economist to assert that, in measuring well-being, what people say about how they feel should be given serious attention. The Commission's advocacy of self-reported well-being is in stark contrast with the behaviorist commandment of the past, and its unambiguous support of subjective measures is especially amazing, given that most of the committee members had been trained in the era of behaviorism. But people do change their minds, even when they've dedicated their research to principles that, like the switchbacks on a well-worn trail, show only one side of the mountain.

"All right," sighs Keaton. "It looks like we're getting there."

15.4   Lionel Robbins Lives On!

But the study of happiness, let alone the happiness-income paradox, has hardly gained universal acceptance in economics, despite the Commission's unequivocal conclusion that interpersonal comparisons provide meaningful data.

"Isn't there always a backlash?" asks Zack, concerned.

Sort of the way things work, isn't it, Zack?

Here's just one example: Rejecting outright a happiness paper by one of my graduate students, the editor of a leading economics journal on public policy recently maintained that.

while the analysis and results [of your paper] are interesting, and, moreover, several papers on "happiness" have been published [in this journal] in the past, I no longer am willing to consider them because the concept violates a fundamental principle of economics ruling out interpersonal comparisons of utility.

Ah, yes…"a fundamental principle of economics!"

By the same token, even though survey evidence is more admissible in economics these days than it was in the 1970s, it is still treated like the new kid on the block, as second-class, "soft" data. A perfect example is the introductory statement in a book review by Nobel Laureate in economics, Ed Prescott: "Being an economist, in this review I focus on the author's sizeable collection of hard statistics, not on opinion polls" (*Economic Journal*, November 2007, p. F648). Note the typical *braggadocio*—"Being an economist"—about the behaviorist approach that disdains what people say and feel. It's as though it's a good thing to go through life wearing blinders.

15.5   Ever Onward!

"So what about social change?" Keaton asks again.

Despite these remnants of the behaviorist era, happiness continues to make progress. A growing number of scholars, as well as the general public, are vitally interested in what people say about their feelings. We're moving toward promising developments on the policy front, Keaton. In 2012, the United Nations organized a conference on happiness, and it now publishes an annual *World Happiness Report*, which contains estimates of happiness for over 150 countries worldwide. (I've referred to some of the findings on country rankings a couple of times in our class.) In 2013, the Secretary-General of the United Nations issued a document encouraging governments to "[use] carefully constructed, regular, large-scale data on happiness and well-being as a more appropriate indicator for improving macroeconomic policymaking and informing service delivery." Following suit, the European Organisation for Economic Cooperation and Development (OECD) has put forth uniform guidelines for the official collection of happiness data. Now, over a dozen governments worldwide are officially collecting happiness statistics.

"The beginnings of the Happiness Revolution, Professor Easterlin??"

References and Further Reading

Blanchflower, D. G., & Oswald, A. J. (2004). Well-being over time in Britain and the USA. *Journal of Public Economics, 88*(7–8), 1359–1386.

Diener, E. (1984). Subjective well-being. *Psychological Bulletin, 95*(3), 542–575.

Fuchs, V. (1983). *How we live.* Cambridge: MA Harvard University Press.

Inglehart, R. (2000). *World values surveys and European values surveys, 1981–1984, 1990–1993, and 1995–1997.* Ann Arbor, MI: Inter-university Consortium for Political and Social Research.

Kahneman, D., & Tversky, A. (1979). Prospect theory: An analysis of decision under risk. *Econometrica, 47*(2), 263–292.

Kuhn, T. S. (1962). *The structure of scientific revolutions.* Chicago: University of Chicago Press.

McCloskey, D. N. (1983). The rhetoric of economics. *Journal of Economic Literature, 21*(2), 481–517.

Oswald, A. J. (1997). Happiness and economic performance. *Economic Journal, 107*(445), 1815–1831.

Robbins, L. (1932). *An essay on the nature and significance of economic science.* London: Macmillan.

Stiglitz, J., Sen, A., & Fitoussi, J. P. (2009). Report by the commission on the measurement of economic performance and social progress. Available at www.stiglitz-sen-fitoussi.fr

Veenhoven, R. (2005). World database of happiness. Available at www.worlddatabaseofhappiness.eur.nl

16

Dream on, Professor!

16.1 Back to the Future: 50 Years On

"I don't know," says Jane doubtfully. "Things look pretty grim to me right now."

"Yeah," agrees Zack. "I have my worries for us."

"What do you think, professor?" asks Lily. "Will the world become a happier place? For us and others, I mean, in our lifetime?"

A big question. But I have a positive take.

When I first started thinking about happiness, as I've said before, my research and teaching were in economic history and demography. So, I look at well-being in light of the history of economic and population change over the last few centuries. I know most of you've had only limited opportunity to acquire much knowledge of history.

"Excuse me, professor, but maybe we know more than you think," Tyler politely interjects. Maybe, and I do hope so, because lack of historical context often results in short-sighted analysis. So, Tyler, perhaps you and the class will help me fill out this background picture.

As I see it, in just under three centuries, we've made three quantum leaps in the human condition—and I mean *quantum, spectacular leaps*. The first long jump was the Industrial Revolution of the late eighteenth century; the second, the Demographic Revolution that began in the late nineteenth; and now a third, the Happiness Revolution, which emerged in the late twentieth century. Lots of revolutions, it's true. But that's the reality of the last three centuries. We've seen the materialization of a world totally different from what went before.

Ada raises her hand shyly.

"My evolutionary psychology professor says this is the biggest transition since human settlements were established, around 10,000 years ago. Do you agree?"

"That is certainly the case, Ada."

"These must be great breakthroughs," says Emma impatiently. "So, what are they?"

16.2   Industrialization: A Revolution in Living Conditions

Let's start with the Industrial Revolution. From our perspective today, living conditions in seventeenth- and eighteenth-century pre-industrial societies, including Europe and America, were little short of camping out, though probably, in truth, less healthy. In the United States, for example, most of the population lived in rural areas, where houses were typically one-story affairs with one or two rooms and no flooring except the hard earth. A fireplace with a chimney was the sole source of heat and doubled as well for cooking. A few windows with shutters but no glass offered ventilation and daylight and candles supplemented the fireplace for light in the evening. No bathroom: Outdoor privies provided for toilet needs. Water and wood had to be fetched. To get from one place to another, walking 5 or 10 miles a day was routine for hardworking country people; other than that, some but not all had a horse and a wagon.

"Ugh," says Zack.

"Yeah," agrees Nancy Ann. "My English professor talks about this stuff all the time. It was gross! She said people died when they were, like, 40 years old. Is that really true, professor?"

It's true that death rates were high. But let's not forget, Nancy Ann, that some people lived relatively long lives. Keep in mind that there was no accepted germ theory until the 1870s. We'll talk more about this shortly.

Now, compare this picture of nearly nonexistent health resources and knowledge and a labor-intensive lifestyle with today's superior hygiene and panoply of consumer goods in industrial societies: multi-room houses with running water, central heating (and often cooling), one or more full bathrooms, electrical appliances, telecommunications and computers, cars and planes, and a phenomenal array of food and clothes. The late Dorothy Brady, a former colleague of mine and a leading economist and economic historian, has said that the average American today lives better than the wealthy did two and a half centuries ago.

Amazing, isn't it, what a couple of centuries has wrought?

You can get a hint of what the more than tenfold multiplication of GDP per capita from 1750 to the present means in terms of our day-to-day lives from today's handout (Table 16.1), which I put together some time ago for my course in economic history. Most of the things that we now take for granted didn't even exist two centuries ago. This is why it is *a revolution*; there has been a total transformation in people's material lives.

"So how did all this happen so suddenly?" Lily asks.

"I know. Urbanization!" says Nancy Ann.

Urbanization is part, a piece, of the answer, but it is, in fact, a result of the real underlying cause which was a radical breakthrough in methods of

Table 16.1 American consumer goods of the 1990s nonexistent or rare two centuries ago (Handout #11)

Household furnishings	Kitchen equipment	Personal care
Electric lighting	Electric/gas range	Eyeglasses
Running water	Electric/gas oven	Contact lenses
Indoor flush toilet	Electric/gas refrigerator	Artificial limbs
Electric/gas hot water heater	Coffee maker	Safety razor
Air conditioning	Microwave oven	Vitamins
Ceiling fan	Dishwasher	Painkillers
Floor coverings	Freezer	Anti-allergenics
Bedsprings	Outdoor gas grill	Anti-depressants
Household cleaning	Toaster	Exercise equipment
Vacuum cleaner	Waffle iron	Quartz, digital watch
Clothes washer	Food processor	Food, tobacco
Clothes dryer	Blender	Canned foods
Electric iron	Friction matches	Frozen foods
Cleaning preparations	Communications	Prepared cereals and mixes
Recreation	Telephone	Margarine
Radio	Cordless phone	Chewing gum
Color television	Answering machine	Cigarettes
Video cassette recorder	Personal computer	Pocket lighter
Stereo equipment	Laser printer	Transportation
Camcorder	Cellular phone	Automobile
Movies	Pager	Jet airplane flight
Motorboat	Fax machine	Bicycle
Jet ski	Photocopier	Motorcycle
Camera	Mechanical pen/pencil	Clothing
		Synthetic fibers
		Sewing machine

production. These new methods often required production to be concentrated in large-scale factories and gave rise to the need for workers in urban centers. Before the Industrial Revolution, ordinary things like clothing, shoes, and household furnishings were made in small shops or at home—so-called cottage industry—mostly with hand tools, and manufacturing was distributed widely in towns and villages across the countryside. The sources of power were humans (pumping a foot treadle on a spinning wheel—Fig. 16.1), animals (pulling a plow), and simple windmills and waterwheels (for milling grain into flour). In the late eighteenth century, inventions in steam power and wrought iron laid the foundation in numerous industries for the development of machine methods of production in large-scale factories (Fig. 16.2), and manufacturing shifted increasingly to urban centers. Wrought iron was made strong and durable machinery possible; steam supplied the robust and stable motive power needed to drive the machinery. Steam and iron also

Fig. 16.1 Eighteenth-century spinning wheel (Credit Radharc images/Alamy Stock Photos)

Fig. 16.2 Spinning shed, nineteenth-century textile factory (Credit: World History Archive/Alamy Stock Photos)

revolutionized transportation through the invention of the railroad and steamboat, effecting efficient freight shipping of goods and enabling passenger transportation, consequently reducing dependence on travel by foot, wagon, coach, and sail.

"OK, so this is great. But it seems to me that information technology is as important as all these other things, you know?" offers Dan.

"Yes, hold on, Dan—we're getting there, but not quite yet."

"If you say so."

We've only just glossed the First Industrial Revolution with these few major examples of production and transportation technology at its core, and we're only halfway through the nineteenth century so far.

"Can you guess what came next, Dan?"

"Um, let's see—Could it be a *Second Industrial Revolution?*"

Exactly so! The Second Industrial Revolution started in the last half of the nineteenth century and further expanded production possibilities. As with the First Industrial Revolution, new breakthroughs in power and industrial materials were its genesis. The invention of the internal combustion engine, which led in time to new transportation systems based on motor vehicles and the airplane as well as to power-driven agricultural tractors, was the first of two breakthroughs in power. The second was the introduction of electric power and the development of a far-flung electric power grid that provided the basis for the electrification of numerous manufacturing industries and agricultural operations. Separately, the raw materials available to firms expanded to encompass steel, nonferrous metals, and eventually plastics and synthetics.

And now, we're in the midst of a Third Industrial Revolution.

"Are we talking IT, information technology?" asks Dan impishly.

Indeed, at last we are, Dan. The digital computer is the catalyst for the Third Industrial Revolution. Now you all probably don't think about factory production when you open your laptops or pull out your cellphones, but once again, factory production along with business methods and organization has been largely transformed. Computers control the equipment and production line in a factory. Computer-programmed robots are replacing workers. Office functions such as document storage, workflow, and supply chain management have witnessed a continuous process of transformation, precipitated by longer and longer strides in computer technology. But IT is not the whole story. Along with the advances in information technology, new sources of power, for example, are being developed. Renewable energy technologies that harness sunlight, wind, and water on a large scale are starting to replace fossil fuels.

These revolutions in production technology over a period of about 250 years, with their sequence of widely applicable productivity-raising inventions, have brought about a total transformation in the everyday living conditions of the average household.

And this kind of massive change is revolutionary, why? It's unprecedented in economic history.

16.3 Next Up: The Demographic Revolution

"Next!" announces Sue.

"Says here 'the demographic revolution,'" Tyler offers, looking at the syllabus.

"Oh, yes," Ada joins in. "We discussed something like that in evo psych, too—the demographic transition. It's when people mysteriously stopped having so many kids."

That's right, all—but perhaps not exactly mysterious. Before the middle of the nineteenth century, many babies died at birth or in infancy and childhood. So, we're circling back to some of the issues Nancy Ann raised earlier about life expectancy, sanitation, and related knowledge and services. Human life expectancy at birth was at best around 40 years or a little more in 1840 and much less in many parts of the world. Today, life expectancy in the highest-ranking countries is more than twice that number, exceeding 80 years, and even the lowest countries, at 50 years or more, are higher than the leading nations of 1840. This remarkable extension of length of life reflects a massive reduction in the death rate and a striking improvement in people's health.

The reduction in deaths—in mortality—was especially concentrated among infants and children, and, in the course of time, this had a major impact on people's child-bearing behavior. In the era of high infant and child mortality, most parents—the elite aside—had as many children as they could, because the prospect of child survival was so uncertain. Of 1000 infants born alive, as many as 200 to 300 would die before their first birthday; and even those who survived the first year still faced a sizable risk of dying before reaching adulthood. Only about one-half of those surviving infancy lived to age 20. Today, in countries leading the way, of 1000 infants born alive, only 5 or less will die in their first year of life, and all but 20 will survive to adulthood.

"Wow, that's great!" enthuses Nancy Ann. "Those poor parents. I'm feeling happier already."

"Geesh," Tyler adds, in agreement. "I don't know any families where a baby died before the first birthday."

"I guess the improvement in life expectancy meant that people had to start looking around for new problems," Sue offers.

Well, the enormous advance in life expectancy was a great achievement, but keep in mind that any drastic change may upend an existing balance in the social system. So, no fear of wasting your time looking for new problems, Sue—they were built right into this remarkable progress. While the substantial decline in infant and childhood deaths is certainly cause for immense celebration, it also radically altered family dynamics, with growing child survival inducing a major change in attitudes toward having children. As infant and child mortality plunged, parents unexpectedly found themselves with larger families and more and more mouths to feed.

Compounding this, industrialization and attendant urbanization replaced much farm labor with factory work, reducing in the course of time the need for extra hands—that is, working children—which had been necessary on family farms. Taken together with child labor laws and mandatory education, introduced in the course of the nineteenth century, this meant that children didn't generally contribute to a family's income. I think we agree that this is another important advance, one stemming from the late eighteenth-century awareness that the childhood years are formative—that children aren't simply undersized adults. But this also means that raising children became progressively more cost- and labor-intensive.

As parents increasingly found themselves with more children than they could support, a growing number began adopting methods to prevent pregnancy. In Europe, which was in the forefront of the mortality decline, parents resorted primarily to traditional but previously seldom-used methods like withdrawal and abstinence, along with the use of condom. These methods proved quite effective in reducing child-bearing. But by the latter half of the twentieth century, new and even more effective contraceptive techniques were developed, including the birth control pill and IUD. In countries leading the Demographic Revolution, birth rates followed death rates—that is, in demographers' terminology, human fertility followed mortality—trending sharply downward throughout much of the twentieth century, except for a transitory post-World War II baby boom. The average number of births per woman dropped from five or more in the late nineteenth century to two or less by 2000. Elsewhere in the world as the decline in mortality took hold, fertility followed suit.

This amazing shift from very high to low levels of mortality, coupled with the ensuing decline from high to low levels of fertility, is usually called the Demographic Transition. However, I prefer the term *Demographic Revolution*, following my late colleague, demographer John Durand. Durand's phrase provides a modification in the direction of precision, because it underscores the sweeping transformation in people's health and length of life, and foregrounds as well a radical alteration in human behavior—the first widespread adoption by parents of deliberate efforts to limit family size.

"So why did so many people die young in the old days?" asks Lily.

"Because they didn't know why people got sick!" Nancy Ann bursts out.

You hit the nail on the head there, Nancy Ann. It's hard to believe these days, but before the mid-nineteenth century, there was very little useful knowledge of the causes, transmission, or treatment of disease. Here's a brief description of the medical care of a Philadelphia tallow chandler in the fall of 1826:

> who complained of chills, pains in the head and back, weakness in the joints and nausea....[B]efore seeing a regular physician he was bled till symptoms of fainting came on. Took an emetic, which operated well. For several days after, kept his bowels moved with Sulph. Soda, Senna tea, etc. He then employed a Physician who prescribed another Emetic, which operated violently and whose action was kept up by drinking bitter tea. (Rosenberg, 1979, 13)

As they say, if the disease doesn't kill you, the cure will. It's hard not to wonder about the efficacy of the main treatments for disease—emetics, cathartics, diuretics, and bleeding—before the Demographic Revolution.

"And they thought miasmas caused disease," says Nancy Ann, in disgust. "Swamp fog."

Yes, that was the prevalent theory throughout much of the nineteenth century. Misguided, but some analysts like mid-nineteenth-century social reformer Edwin Chadwick did see in this theory a good reason for the need for cleaner water and better spacing of housing, especially in urban areas. The work of Chadwick and others was the stimulus for the "sanitation revolution," a mid-nineteenth-century movement to clean up the cities that proved in time remarkably successful. And then, in the latter third of the nineteenth century, thanks to scientists such as Louis Pasteur and Robert Koch, the germ theory finally triumphed over miasmatic theory. Medical science began to pinpoint the sources of infectious disease and devise techniques for its prevention.

"Hopefully, it wasn't as dangerous to go to the doctor by then," Andy remarks.

"Yeah," agrees Zack.

Yes, I think we'd all agree on that, though until the 1940s, the contribution of doctors was largely limited to diagnosing and perhaps moderately alleviating one's illness with drugs. There was little they could do to cure disease. Progress in the control of infectious disease, like the remarkable industrial changes we've seen, resulted from successive strides in technology—again, three of them, and therapy, the availability of cures, came last. The first started with Chadwick's sanitation revolution and consisted of new methods to prevent the transmission of disease, based on discoveries of the carriers of infection—contaminated air and water, insects, and rodents. Historians of science usually credit Dr. John Snow's linkage of cholera to a contaminated water supply in 1854 as a breakthrough discovery. The second leap forward, which began in the latter part of the nineteenth century, was propelled by research validating the germ theory of disease and by the ensuing development of vaccines to prevent diseases like diphtheria, pertussis, tetanus, and yellow fever.

"I know what the third one was," Ryder announces. "Antibiotics."

"He's right," says Nancy Ann. "People used to die of stuff like strep throat."

Yes, you're both right, but don't get carried away. Most of the remarkable decline in mortality was due to the sanitation revolution and the development of vaccines which vastly reduced the transmission and spread of infectious disease. Although Alexander Fleming discovered penicillin in 1928 (Fig. 16.3), it remained pretty much a laboratory curiosity until 1939 when Howard Florey and Ernst Chain established its lifesaving possibilities. (All three shared the Nobel Prize in 1945.) And even then, the large-scale production needed for wartime and eventually civilian use was not accomplished until near the

Fig. 16.3 Alexander Fleming (Credit: GL Archive/Alamy Stock Photos)

end of World War II. But the amazing success of penicillin in treating bacterial infections led in time to the subsequent development of numerous other antibiotic medications.

"Well, I guess the doctors were really happy about antibiotics," Emma says.

"Hardly," Ryder counters. "There's always a new problem."

Right, and right again. For the first time doctors had the power to cure disease, endowed, in effect, with powers equivalent to divine intervention, and their social status soared.

Some scholars, ignorant of viral infections, proclaimed the eventual elimination of infectious disease. And so, attention turned to a new problem, as Ryder says. In the latter half of the twentieth century, medical research increasingly shifted from infectious disease, which disproportionately impacted the young, to conditions of older age. In consequence, in the last 70 years or so, medicine has made significant advances in reducing deaths from heart disease and stroke; in the treatment and control of high blood pressure, high cholesterol, and some cancers; and in coronary surgery.

"I bet you're glad about that," comments Ted.

You bet! My generation does indeed benefit, but even more significantly, the subsequent large cohort born after World War II.

"The baby boomers!"

You've got it: The so-called baby boomers and their children and grandchildren, including all of you, face longer and higher quality of life into old age.

"Everybody wins!" Andy shouts.

16.4   Timing and Geographic Diffusion

"Well, that's all great for Europe and the United States," remarks Jill. "But what about India and Africa, places like that?"

There are lags in the timing and geographic spread of these advances, certainly. In the parts of the world that were first to modernize, the Demographic Revolution lagged the Industrial Revolution by almost a century. But the way in which each spread throughout the world was similar. In broad outline, both started in Western Europe and spread southward and eastward across the face of Europe. A roughly concurrent expansion took place in overseas offshoots of Europe, places where European migrants settled in substantial numbers—Northern America, parts of Latin America, and Oceania. Next came the developing nations in Asia, the rest of Latin America and Northern Africa, and, finally, sub-Saharan Africa. But note that, although the Demographic Revolution started a century later than the Industrial Revolution, it spread throughout the world much more rapidly, and, in fact, in sub-Saharan Africa, it has preceded the Industrial Revolution.

"How could that be?" wonders Lily.

"Yeah, wasn't it a regular pattern?" asks Owen.

So, let's see how this all fits into place. First, the geographic spread of the two Revolutions around the world was so similar because Western Europe and, in time, its offshoots, were the principal sources of the great underlying breakthroughs in production and biomedical technology, gradually extending outward from the primary source. Once the basic knowledge had been acquired and applied, modernization processes accelerate. But they don't do so completely systematically, Lily, because economics factors into the relative speed of the spread of these revolutions. In a nutshell, because the cost of controlling infectious disease is relatively low compared to that of promoting economic growth, the Demographic Revolution spread much more rapidly than the Industrial Revolution, and this is why it ends up leading the two in sub-Saharan Africa.

Don't the timing and diffusion make sense, then, once you account for the cost factors?

"Yes, they do," Lily agrees.

16.5 Tracing the Source: The Scientific Revolution

"O.K." Sue throws down her backpack. "Is today the review session?"

"Says here 'The Scientific Revolution,'" Tyler replies, scanning his syllabus.

"No! Not another!" gasps Ted. "I'm starting to forget about happiness."

"Well I think it's interesting," says Ada, blushing.

Thank you, Ada—I'm happy to have you in my camp!

And this is the daddy of them all. The Scientific Revolution of the seventeenth century is the bedrock of all the other revolutions, because it introduces a new and highly successful approach to the acquisition of knowledge that marks the beginning of modern science. The advances of the Industrial and Demographic Revolutions were due, at bottom, to the emergence of modern science and the growth of empirically tested scientific knowledge in Western Europe and its offshoots.

We have all come of age in a world so dominated by science that we take its presence for granted. But before the seventeenth century, the sciences as we know them today did not exist, and inquiries into the physical world fell under the heading of "natural philosophy." In the Victorian era, Charles Darwin and Alfred Russel Wallace, for example, the fathers of evolution by natural selection, were not called "biologists" but "naturalists." The term "scientist" itself did not appear until the nineteenth century and only slowly gained traction.

"Yes, but they were scientists, no matter what they were called," Ada insists.

Very true—but before them, the efficacy of repeated observation as the foundation of knowledge wasn't firmly established.

The Scientific Revolution began in Western Europe in the seventeenth century with a drastic shift in the approach to learning about the world around us. Turning away from the traditional method of a priori deduction and toward an empirical and experimental approach, researchers developed, for the first time, the techniques and process that lead to valid scientific knowledge: hypothesis, observation through controlled experimentation, proof (or disproof), experimental iteration, theory, reiteration, further proof, and, in many cases, practical application.

"Actually, professor, the method had its roots in classical Greece."

"Yeah. Aristotle!" says Nancy Ann.

Very true. But although this empirical approach was championed in ancient Greece—most notably by Aristotle, as Nancy Ann points out—it did not take hold anywhere as a principal method of discovery until practiced and promoted in Europe in the seventeenth century by such figures as Johannes Kepler, Galileo, Rene Descartes, Isaac Newton, and William Harvey.

The first scientific fields to emerge were in the natural sciences—astronomy and mechanics in the sixteenth and seventeenth centuries, followed by chemistry in the eighteenth and electricity and thermodynamics in the nineteenth. Developments in these fields established the foundational knowledge for the inventions that fueled the Industrial Revolution. Cause and effect went in both directions. Thus, James Watt's invention of the modern steam engine antedated and furthered the development of thermodynamics, but thermodynamics, once established, was in turn responsible for major improvements in the steam engine. Both scientific discoveries and inventions were the product of the new methods of inquiry of the Scientific Revolution.

"You haven't said anything about biology," Ryder reminds me.

The life sciences, including biology, which study living organisms, took somewhat longer to develop than the natural sciences and didn't take off until the nineteenth century. Why is this so, Ryder? In both astronomy and mechanics, the two fields in which the Scientific Revolution first occurred, the basic phenomena were largely matters of everyday observation.

"Oh, right," Ryder agrees. "We needed the tools."

"You know, those Enlightenment philosophers in the seventeenth and eighteenth century talked about the limits of human sense perception," Dan informs us, "just at the same time they were changing method. John Locke, David Hartley, and David Hume. For instance—".

Exactly! In the biological fields, scientific advance had to wait on the development of increasingly sophisticated instruments like the optical microscope and its successors. These extend the range and observational efficacy of human perception, as Dan's suggesting. Building on this, the biological sciences developed in close association with the public health and medical advances of the nineteenth century, and all were collectively the driving force behind the Demographic Revolution. Thus, the Demographic Revolution lagged the Industrial Revolution because of the later emergence of the life sciences compared with the natural sciences.

"So why don't we learn this stuff in history class?" asks Sue. "I'm a history major, for heaven's sake. We never learn any of this."

Well—

"You have to study it in philosophy, or history and sociology of science," Dan informs her. "Actually—"

"So excuse me, but I learned a bunch about it in English class," Nancy Ann adds. "Romantic poetry. Blake. Anna Laetitia Barbauld. Wordsworth. Stuff like that."

You see that, class? Look at what we get when we pool our knowledge from our various primary interests. I had a whole, multi-part lecture here for you—and a pretty good one, I must admit—and yet, I still learn something new from my students every day!

16.6   The Happiness Revolution

"Our last class!" says Lily.

"Says here 'the Happiness Revolution.'" Tyler points to his syllabus.

"So, once we wrap this up, do we have our review session?" asks Sue. "I mean, all very interesting, but I want to do well on the exam. That'll make *me* happy!"

There'll be time for that, most definitely, Sue—but I'm pretty confident that you've all pieced it together by now.

Here it is: The Happiness Revolution.

Whereas the two prior revolutions, the Industrial Revolution and the Demographic Revolution, led to a transformation in people's *objective* circumstances, as indexed by the multiplication of real GDP per capita and life expectancy, the principal concern of the Happiness Revolution is different and calls for a different kind of measure. Which is?

"What people have to say about themselves," Andy offers. "Specifically, people's feelings about their lives as a whole."

Yes! This revolution centers on people's feelings—how happy they are and how satisfied with their lives. It becomes a revolution, the Happiness Revolution, when the findings show a marked improvement in people's *feelings* of well-being, i.e., their *subjective* well-being. And this is what's happening now!

The first two revolutions, the Industrial Revolution and the Demographic Revolution, resulted from the rise of the natural and life sciences. The Happiness Revolution is the product of the social sciences. Economics was the first of the social sciences, emerging in the latter half of the eighteenth century in the work of Adam Smith. But formal teaching and research disciplines in the social sciences—economics, sociology, political science, anthropology, and psychology—had to wait on the secularization of universities toward the latter part of the nineteenth century before they could be established. It was only then that institutions of higher education increasingly turned away from their traditional orientation toward classical and religious studies.

"And also, there were new kinds of knowledge from around the world, things about culture and myth. Sir James Fraser." Nancy Ann frowns.

"Yes," says Keaton. "And you need to start valuing all humans and their differences before people will care enough to study them. That's the only way you have those research areas and start getting meaningful social change."

I think you're making an important point about values and their impact on the content of higher education. All of the social science disciplines address the patterns and dynamics of human life and culture, and these wouldn't have entered the curricula as worthy areas of study unless a large number of folks found them interesting and valuable. What's more, a commitment to human well-being undergirds most of the social sciences, though perhaps this commitment has been, since their inception, often implied rather than overtly expressed.

"Never too late for change," Keaton observes.

Interdisciplinary research in the social sciences provides the robust foundation for the Happiness Revolution. Some measures, like GDP and life expectancy, relate primarily to specific social sciences—in this case, to economics and demography, respectively. By contrast, happiness is a concept recognized across the social sciences. It reflects the things universally important for people's lives. After the previous century's proliferation of social science disciplines, the current study of happiness is bringing the various human fields of study back into conversation with one another, focused on the goal of human well-being.

The first and foremost achievement of the social sciences has been to establish widespread public recognition that circumstances like unemployment, poor health, and poverty are mostly the result of forces beyond an individual's control and that collective action is required to help those suffering from such circumstances. Before the twentieth century, the common belief was that these problems were the result of an individual's character flaws—laziness, failure to save, dirtiness, drunkenness, gambling, and the like.

"Yeah, Victorians believed in the deserving and the undeserving poor," Nancy Ann chips in.

Notions like these were bolstered by a hierarchical concept of human reality, which held that some persons were, by virtue of their birth, better than others. Economics initially supported such beliefs through its advocacy of laissez-faire, maintaining that government should be small and that to intervene in people's lives would only promote dependency. The laissez-faire view eroded progressively, however, because of the persistence of grinding poverty and the emergence of severe financial crises and major depressions. The rise of democratic individualism and the middle class further undermined the ethos of laissez-faire.

As the problems of the free market economy became clearer, the developing social sciences put forward two major strands of solutions, directed respectively toward employment and the social safety net. Policies on the economic side were aimed at stabilizing the economy at high levels of employment: first, via the establishment in the early twentieth century of central banks responsible for monetary policy and then, in response to the Great Depression of the 1930s, fiscal policy. Fiscal policy was the discovery of how to use central government taxing and spending policies to fight recessions, on the one hand, and control rapid inflation, on the other.

Around the same time, social policy started to take formal shape.

"Hurrah!" shouts Keaton.

As I way saying, social policy started to take formal shape, resulting in a set of programs we now call the "social safety net." We have already talked about the safety net in many of our discussions here. It consists of programs encompassing such things as income support (unemployment insurance, social security, social assistance, and disability benefits), health care, infant and childcare, education (including preschool programs), maternity and paternity leave, elder care, and old-age pensions. Today's Nordic welfare states have most fully realized these policy initiatives and programs.

"So, no use for GDP?" asks Zack.

A useful figure, as we've said, for certain things, but GDP and economic growth, for which it serves as a measure, do not feature in the Happiness Revolution specifically. Although the Industrial Revolution resulted, on average, in a vast improvement in people's material lives, there is no evidence, as we've learned, that economic growth in itself increases people's happiness. To the contrary, the shift to a free market economy that promotes economic growth leads to stress and uncertainty about jobs, income, health care, and family circumstances—things that we've seen over and over again are critical to happiness. The cradle-to-grave safety net addresses these concerns. Most notably, less-advantaged people particularly report greater happiness as a result of safety net policies.

"Hurrah again!" exclaims Keaton.

Yes, indeed—hurrah again! Our measures of subjective well-being, not GDP, capture a nation's success in addressing the things most important to people in all walks of life, the everyday concerns that speak to their happiness.

Summing up, as with its predecessors, the Happiness Revolution originated in Western Europe. The Nordic countries, who were in the forefront of introducing and developing welfare state policies, have become the world leaders in happiness, and similar policies are now gradually spreading throughout the world.

"Victors in the Happiness Revolution!" Keaton pronounces.

Well, "Leaders" would be better, because happily!—untold numbers can win.

16.7   Back to the Future, Again

So, that's it!

Considered in historical perspective, the Industrial Revolution is, at bottom, the product of the natural sciences; the Demographic Revolution, the fruit of the life sciences; and the Happiness Revolution, the creation of the social sciences. Although there is some interdependence, each revolution, based as it is on a distinctive body of scientific knowledge, is largely independent of the others.

The sequence in the occurrence of the three revolutions reflects the progression in the emergence and growth of knowledge since the Scientific Revolution of the seventeenth century–from natural sciences to life sciences to social sciences. In each area of science, there has been a continuous interplay between basic and applied knowledge; both are products of the scientific method that originated with the Scientific Revolution. All three revolutions have followed a similar path of diffusion throughout the world, starting in Western Europe, the birthplace of the underlying scientific knowledge, and spreading outward from there.

What do you think, Zack? A little less worried about the future in the face of this broader perspective?

"Yes, definitely, a little less worried. Thank you."

"Well," says Jill. "You make it sound inevitable."

Hmm—maybe not inevitable. But I believe it will come. And you, my dear class, are the beneficiaries of all three revolutions!

References and Further Reading

Easterlin, R. A. (1996). *Growth triumphant: The twenty-first century in historical perspective*. Ann Arbor, MI: University of Michigan Press.

Easterlin, R. A. (2004). *The reluctant economist: Perspectives on economics, economic history, and demography*. Cambridge, UK: Cambridge University Press.

Easterlin, R. A. (2019). Three revolutions of the modern era. *Comparative Economic Studies, 61*(4), 521–530.

Lindberg, D. C. (1992). *The beginnings of western science: The European scientific tradition in philosophical, religious, and institutional context, 600 B. C. to A. D. 1450*. Chicago: University of Chicago Press.

Rosenberg, C. E. (1979). The therapeutic revolution: Medicine, meaning, and social change in nineteenth-century America. In M. J. Vogel & C. E. Rosenberg (Eds.), *The therapeutic revolution* (pp. 3–25). Philadelphia: University of Pennsylvania Press.

Glossary

Behaviorism The belief that scientific understanding of people's behavior is obtained from focusing on what they do, not what they say.

Cohort Persons born in the same year.

Consumer sovereignty Ability of consumers to dispose of income as they wish, free from external restrictions like government taxation or regulation.

Cross-section data An array of statistics for a given point in time, typically a specific year.

Decision utility The satisfaction expected from a particular choice.

Domain satisfaction The satisfaction relating to a particular aspect of one's life (finances, health, etc.).

Economic growth Sustained long-term uptrend in real GDP per capita.

EU European Union.

Evaluative well-being Satisfaction with one's overall state-of-life.

Experienced utility The satisfaction realized from a particular choice.

Experiential well-being One's satisfaction (mood) at the current or recent time.

Fallacy of composition The belief that what is true for the individual is also true for the "whole," the group of persons of which the individual is a part.

GDP The nation's annual output of goods and services.

GDP per capita GDP on a per person basis, a rough approximation to a nation's average income per person.

Happiness One's overall feelings of well-being.

Income Money used to fund all expenditures, including savings, taxes, and transfers to others (e.g., gifts).

Income reference level An individual's internal benchmark used to assess how satisfactory is one's actual income.

© The Author(s), under exclusive license to Springer Nature Switzerland AG 2021
R. A. Easterlin, *An Economist's Lessons on Happiness*,
https://doi.org/10.1007/978-3-030-61962-6

Interpersonal comparison Comparison of one's situation with that of others.

Interpersonal comparison of utility Comparing the self-reported satisfaction of different persons on the assumption that their satisfaction is commensurate.

Intrapersonal comparison Comparison of one's current situation with one's personal best.

Ladder-of-life A scale on which respondents rank their happiness from 0 or 1, the lowest rung, up to 10, the highest.

Life cycle (life course) The span of years from youth to old age.

Life satisfaction How satisfied one is with one's life, all things considered.

Longitudinal study An analysis that follows the same persons over time.

Objective data Statistics about an individual not based on self-reports.

Objective well-being Objective data such as income assumed to index a person's feelings of happiness/satisfaction.

OECD Organisation for Economic Cooperation and Development.

Panel study See longitudinal study.

Reference levels The internal benchmarks in terms of which one assesses different life circumstances. See, e.g., income reference level.

Reliability Consistency of an individual's self-reports on a daily or weekly basis.

Safety net A set of policies aimed at ameliorating the typical person's principal cradle-to-grave concerns.

Self-report Information about oneself provided by an individual.

Setpoint In psychology the underlying happiness level of an individual fixed by genes and personality.

Social comparison See interpersonal comparison.

Subjective data Individual statistics obtainable only via self-reports.

Subjective well-being A person's feelings of happiness or life satisfaction, all things considered.

Time-series data Statistics collected at successive points in time, e.g., via annual surveys.

Utility Satisfaction, happiness.

Validity Truthfulness of self-reports of happiness.

Zero-sum game A situation where the gains and losses of participants sum to zero.

Index

Printed in the United States
By Bookmasters